Unravel

by

Rachel CM Jones

Title: Unravel – How to Untangle your mind, craft your plan and actually get things done!

First published in October 2018

The author expressly disclaims any liability, loss or risk which is incurred as a consequence, directly or indirectly, of the use and application of any contents of this work.

ISBN 978-1-9165038-0-9

Editing: Rachel CM Jones
Cover design: Abi Lemon, Brand Pharmacy
(www.brandpharmacy.co.uk)
Interior Graphics: Rachel CM Jones, using Canva

Copyright © 2018 Rachel CM Jones

The right of Rachel CM Jones to be identified as the author of this work has been asserted in accordance with The Copyright Designs and Patents Act 1988.

DEDICATION

To all the Joneses in my life who inspired me to be someone to keep up with.

WHAT PEOPLE ARE SAYING

Read this book if you want practical, step-by-step advice in accomplishing success for you. Packed with loads of personal examples from the author that are easy to identify with. Ideal reading if you need help achieving the one thing you have always put off!

Sarah McGowan, Programme Manager

It's a beautiful thing to have a head full of dreams and ideas. It's admirable to want to turn them into reality and it takes courage to decide to take action but once that decision is made, then what..?! Turning those dreams and ideas into reality can be a challenge. In fact, unravelling those thoughts so you even have a place to start, let alone clear steps to move steadily forward, is much harder than it sounds! It's also much more exciting! Instead of dreams and ideas, it becomes real life... YOUR real life! That has been the most exciting part of my own journey so far... turning the chaos in my mind into something ordered and stepping into what I once thought was beyond my capabilities one small action at a time. Whatever it is, big or small, Rachel has the ability to help you find the clarity and direction you need to move forward. Her humour and straight-talk will have you laughing and nodding along in agreement as you begin to devise your very own game plan.

Joy Hopgood-Gravett, Founder of House of Little Miracles *(championing education support for children affected by prenatal exposure to alcohol).*

I am sure many of you have gotten stuck, overwhelmed, or even at an impasse in life. Getting yourself out of such a situation is no easy task. Maybe you were suddenly made redundant and don't know what to do next, maybe you're stuck in a job you hate and cannot figure a way out. In this book Rachel provides a simple step by step method to help you unravel your thoughts in order for you to produce plans to move you forward to your life goals. Rachel also shows you how to keep track, adjust your plan, and how to deal with disaster. The advice in this book doesn't just help you work through immediate challenges, Rachel's method also help with planning your daily life, and dealing with you own worst enemy….yourself.

Liam Hook, Head of HSE Consultancy Services

CONTENTS

FOREWORD

Let's face it, we all have unfinished projects, plans that remain nothing more than ideas and ambition that fails to become reality. Often the reason behind this fact is that we fail to gain clarity of our current situation, avoid becoming focused on the planned outcome and remain in confusion on the journey to get there.

This set of circumstances is so familiar that I can imagine that you and almost everyone near you at this moment has experienced the frustration of feeling stuck and confused, not knowing where to apply themselves. The confusion being discussed is often perceived as procrastination, fear or sheer laziness yet rarely is this the case.

Our truth is that most people live complex lives with a plethora of choices and a skill rarely refined in the education sector or in life in general is the skill of decision making.

You, me and every other human is equipped with the power of choice. It is these choices that define us and the world that we create for ourselves. It was the great Peter Parker (AKA Spiderman) that famously said, "With great power comes great responsibility" and for you, in your life, your super power is the ability to decide how you choose to apply yourself to achieve your version of success.

The fact that you have decided to read this book

tells me that you are looking to improve your ability to make the decisions to craft your next steps. You are not lazy, you hate to procrastinate and you are ready to use your courage to make a big change. Rachel Jones is an incredible example who has done exactly that, time and time again and more than just a master of detangling complex situations for herself and crafting a positive outcome, she has a magnitude of experience of helping people and organizations achieve the same.

It was my experience of watching Rachel first hand help others to unpack their troubles and neatly rearrange them into manageable steps that was possibly the catalyst for the creation of this book. Despite all her talents and experience, Rachel is not an experienced author, nor has regularly written for people like you, the mastery in this book is that itself is a product of its product. You are physically holding a piece of evidence that the advice shared in Unravel works. It's the processes and principles shared in here that are responsible for the completion of thousands of giant corporate projects, hundreds of individuals' personal successes and the realization of a simple idea in a phone conversation becoming this wonderful book should give you the confidence to let Rachel help you to lead your change.

Phil M Jones

Bestselling Author of Exactly What to Say, Exactly How to Sell and Exactly Where to Start

INTRODUCTION

2004. 1pm on a Wednesday afternoon.

I had just returned from lunch. My manager put a white envelope on my desk as he walked briskly past. It had a post-it note stuck to the front which read "Do not open yet. My office 1.15pm." I knew what was coming. Sure enough, 15 minutes later my manager was intently studying everything else in his office apart from me as he confirmed I was being made redundant. The white envelope contained two copies of my redundancy package - one for me to keep, the other to sign and hand back to him. I felt more sorry for him than for myself as this was clearly not something he was comfortable with. "When from?" was my only question. He dug a box out from under his desk and handed it to me. "Today. You will be on garden leave for your notice period. I need to escort you out by 2pm." I took the box and headed back to my desk. Sympathetic faces watched me pack the last 3 years of my career into a box. A few goodbyes later and I was in my car driving to pick my baby son up early from nursery, feeling a strange sense of elation.

Elation after being made redundant? Let me roll back a bit to explain.

I have always been an intelligent and highly organised person but in the past was also incredibly shy and lacking in self-confidence. I learnt to gain approval from my peers by using my skills primarily to help them. I was the kid at school who did homework assignments early so I had time to help others with theirs; the one who always organised group events so I could be sure of an invite; the one who everyone said could make a success of anything she chose to do but who couldn't decide which direction she wanted her life to go in as she was scared making a decision that lost her some of that approval. In short, I had spent so much time looking to others' needs ahead of my own that I got lost in all that busyness. I soldiered on regardless though and achieved a good degree from a good university, made some good friends, moved to a new city to embark on my career and met and married my amazing husband. Life was bumbling along but it was, well, fine. I had hoped for more. I squashed any feelings of dissatisfaction down and counted my blessings because that's what people do, right? My university friends were going on to achieve great things - travelling the world, getting PhDs, high-flying careers - and whilst I was happy for them, their success was making me feel miserable as I knew deep down that I wasn't fulfilling my own potential. So I reverted to what I had done before - I put my hand up at work for more responsibility, and offered to help colleagues and friends, again to seek fulfilment through approval from others. This sort of worked but the flipside of this was that I was doing far too much, and I was under enormous pressure to get it all done. I was finding out the hard way that I couldn't tackle everything on my plate by just working harder   My home life suffered. My job involved staying away from home 4-5 nights a week most weeks so weekends were a blur of travelling home and then getting ready to travel again. I was putting weight on with a constant diet of hotel food. Our house was a disorganised mess with much-needed home improvement projects taking such a long time to complete as I was away so much. I wanted to be at home more with my husband and actually have time to do things together that weren't housework, laundry or DIY!

Something had to give. What gave was me.

I became a ball of stress - tired all the time but unable to sleep, crying at the drop of a hat, utterly frazzled. Guilt my constant companion. I had lost confidence in my ability to actually get anything done as I was juggling so much.   I realised I needed to do something different but could not get off the merry-go-round of constant bustle and stress. In 2003 all that changed as we welcomed our first son into the world. Although this was an amazingly joyous time, it was also like someone had thrown a hand-grenade into our lives (as any first-time parent can tell you!). Adding a newborn baby to the mix pretty quickly highlights the parts of your life that are on shaky ground. In my case I found that despite still being Mrs Organised in my working life, I was applying none of those skills at home. Zero!

I had been turning a blind eye to our lack of routine, lack of planning and lack of direction but could do so no longer. Living in chaos was possible for a couple but unthinkable with a baby. Our house was a mess - a fixer-upper that wasn't fixed up yet. We were spending a fortune at the supermarket but we never seemed to have anything in the house to eat. We knew we would need to move if we had another child but had no savings. The amount of travelling made my job untenable with a young family so what on earth was going to happen once my maternity leave ended? Suddenly being responsible for the wellbeing of a mini-human, and no desire for yet another 2am trip to the 24hour supermarket for nappies or baby milk, tends to sharpen even the most frazzled of minds!

My husband and I both realised we needed to do something before we both broke. Blessed with several months at home on maternity leave I started to think, then to plan and then to do the things we needed to start turning our lives around.

It worked.

I applied the skills I used every day in my day job to my personal life and slowly but surely turned it around. Within a year we had put routines in place that allowed us to be more organised and free-up both time and money. This had enabled us to complete the larger home improvement projects (just in time for our son reaching the crawling stage), start to build up some savings and gave me time to think about my career direction. Being made redundant a couple of months after my return to work was a bonus as I had already had time to map out my next career move, and I got a much better job (with no travel!) within a month of leaving my old one. Result!

I found that I had developed a particular method of approaching and successfully working through every challenge that I had faced. I had started to treat each one of them like a puzzle to be solved instead of a problem. Like with any puzzle, I unpicked and untangled the threads of the problem so that I could get to its root. Once I knew what the root was, I knew I could find a way to resolve it. To make this more fun for myself, I started calling these challenges 'Projects'. For me, the word Project conjures up something that is both exciting and attainable rather than using terms like goal, target, problem or challenge. I feel that the words goal and target suggest something you can have a go at but missing would be a valid outcome of taking a shot at the goal or target - not exactly the strongest starting point for success. In a similar way, I found that continuing to label what I was working on as a problem or as a challenge was just reiterating to my brain that this is something that is still difficult, despite all my efforts, and it was much more likely to make me think about quitting. If I have a Project to work on then I know that by setting myself up to start the Project and then diligently working through my plan, my chances of success are much, much higher.

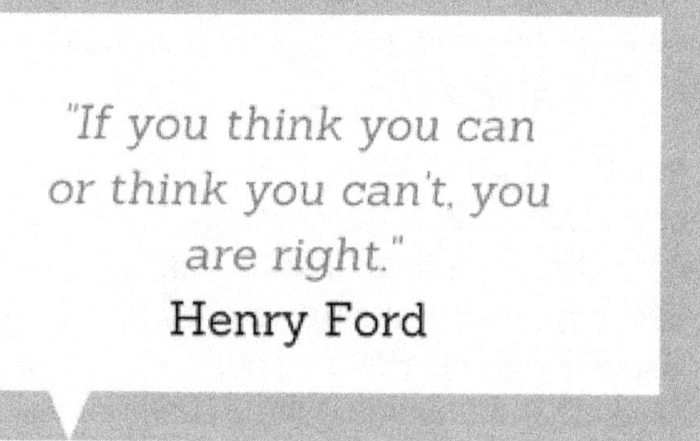

I don't know about you but when I find something that works for me, I keep using it. Every time I have been presented with a challenge or have felt like I was getting stuck again in some aspect of my life I have used the same techniques that I am sharing with you in this book. Following this simple process for nearly 15 years has allowed me to have a successful career, equally successful home life and, more importantly, create the time and space to do things that I have always wanted to do. In my professional life, I have used these skills to forge a successful career in project management. In my personal life, I have created Projects to plan my way into new career paths and new industries, as well as Projects for personal growth.

The growth in my own personal confidence and self-trust has been massive and has enabled me to overcome the chronic shyness I suffered from since childhood and do some things I didn't think were possible for people like me - raising thousands for charity, going from couch to Everest Base Camp and to become an author. On a more mundane level, I use exactly the same techniques in my life every single day to juggle my career, side businesses, family and home commitments and volunteering - whilst still having time to sit down and relax with my husband and sons. Living in this way has become normal to me. I firmly believe that once you know exactly what you want to do, achieving it is simply a matter of creating a plan and taking consistent action - that is what will reward you with success.

Have you ever felt like a failure because you are trying to juggle too many things? Is there something you have always wanted to do but you can't seem to find the time to do it? Do you sometimes find yourself stuck in your own head, over-thinking what you could and should be doing but doubting you will ever actually do any of it? Maybe you feel like there is something wrong with you for not being able to figure this out on your own? All of these lead to procrastination, feelings of guilt and hopelessness that anything will change. I have been there many, many times and each time used this process to get myself moving forward again. I have shared my methods with friends and colleagues and watched them succeed. I have had coaching clients go on to gain the confidence to start new businesses, follow new career paths and make space in their lives for the things that are important to them. Whatever it is you are struggling with, you will need to learn to think in a new way and develop some new skills to get unstuck and allow you to move forward. This is where this book can help you.

In this book I will take you through my 4-step process to help you:

1. Unravel your problem, create clarity and turn it into a Project,

2. Create a plan for your Project,

3. Make space in your life to deliver your Project,

4. Set yourself up for success.

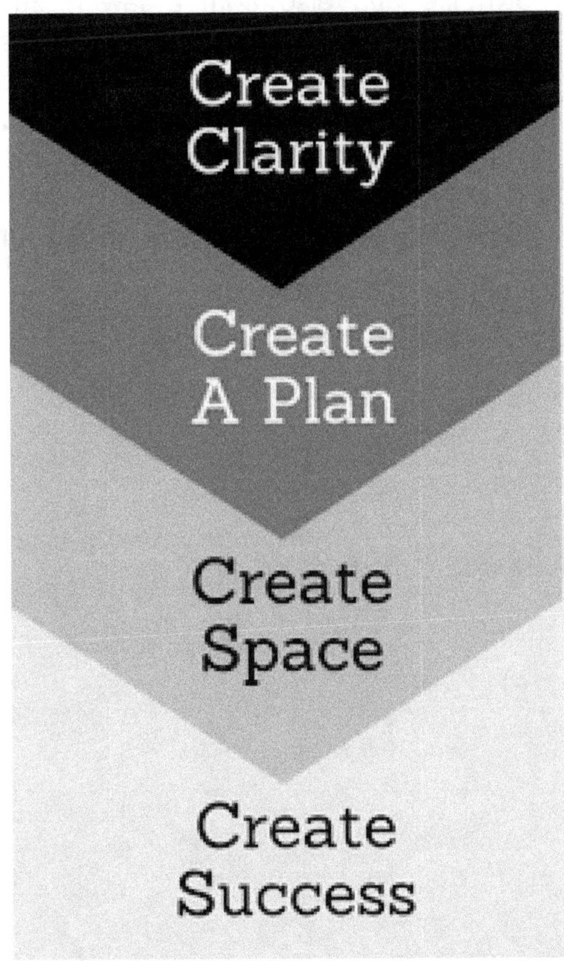

This book is not focused on just believing you can or on positive thinking, instead it is a practical step-by-step guide to show you how to actually start doing the right things to achieve your goals. As we go through this book together, I will share stories from my own life and also from a few of my coaching clients so you can see how the steps work when put into practice. Remember, you need to do the work - this process works but only if you do. If you are ready to take action then let me show you how to follow my process so you can achieve something that makes you proud of yourself.

Ready to go? Good! Let's get cracking!

CREATE CLARITY

1 UNRAVELLING

I had cleared a space at the table, armed myself with pen and paper and metaphorically rolled up my sleeves ready to start sorting my life out. Trouble was I had so much going on in my head that I had no idea where to start. In two minutes my brain had rattled through house / health / money / job / food / baby / what's on tv / what time is it / garden / kitchen / mess / clutter / shopping / dinner on what seemed like an endless loop. How on earth was I going to fix all that?

I could feel myself getting disheartened so decided just to start writing things down as they popped into my head. I ended up writing for over an hour. Just getting everything out of my head so I could see it on the paper in front of me had changed my mood entirely. I found I could actually think clearly for the first time in ages. I didn't realise it at the time but I had just found step one of my process.

Capture the Strands

The first step towards getting clear on what you need to tackle is always to get all the maelstrom of thoughts swirling around in your brain out of your head so you can look at them properly. The single best way I have found to do this is to write it all down. In order to capture your thoughts in writing you have to be able to understand them enough to put the right words to them. The act of writing them has two benefits: your thoughts become something tangible that you can work with, and you gain some head space to enable you to think more clearly. When I am working out how to tackle a new challenge, I always start by doing a "braindump".

If you aren't familiar with the term, a braindump is essentially a big list of everything in your head - you dump all of your thoughts out of your brain and onto the paper. This can be stuff that is bothering you about doing it, things you think you might need to think about and random things your brain decides are worth focusing on at the time. Everything that is on your mind at the time you sit down to write all goes down onto the list.

Try this for yourself - take a piece of paper and start to jot down your thoughts into a list of bullet points. I often find that I start out with just points related to my challenge but that then extends to other things that are on my mind. If you are finding the same, that is perfectly fine. Get it all out onto the page. Really take some time to do this properly. Don't skimp on the detail. Don't try and limit your list to what you think is relevant. Don't try to jump ahead into "solution mode" - focus only on capturing what actually is rather what you think you can do to fix it. If this ends up being more like a journaling session or a jumbled essay as you get into the flow, don't worry about it at this stage.

If the thought of a blank page staring at you is overwhelming and you feel like you don't even know where to begin with jotting your thoughts down, you may find it easier to start with some initial structure to help you guide your thinking. Starting to think of your problem in terms of how it impacts different parts of your life may be useful. For example, is it impacting your finances, career, home, family, friends or health? See what comes to mind around each of these categories. You can then add in other categories and sub-categories as needed as you start to get into it and your thoughts start to flow.

Find the Facts

As you are writing your braindump list, you may find that the things you have captured will be fairly vague statements (e.g. I want to sort my disaster of a house out) which is pretty normal. What is also pretty normal is that many people take that vague statement and try to use that as the basis for what they try to go on to fix. They jump ahead too soon and are doomed to fail. What those people do not appreciate is that there is really only one thing that you need to know in order to begin to solve any problem, face any challenge, or indeed achieve any goal. This is the single most important piece of advice I can give you and it is crucial that we nail this right at the start.

Before you can begin to solve a problem, you need to know exactly what that problem is.

Sounds like a pretty basic step, right?

At this point, you might be thinking to yourself that this is blindingly obvious. You know exactly what your particular problem is. Bear with me for a few moments. Before you decide to skip this part and try a later section, I invite you to just spend a few moments considering this point. Have you ever dived right in on taking action towards something and put your heart and soul into it only to end up disappointed in yourself as you aren't getting the results you expect? Did you find yourself losing focus, losing drive, giving up and ultimately feeling like you had failed?

In my experience, the main reason most people struggle to overcome their problem is that they have not taken the time to really get to the heart of what they are trying to resolve. They jump into action with only a superficial understanding of what they are trying to do and invariably end up trying to

> "An hour of planning
> can save ten hours of
> doing."
> Dale Carnegie

fix the wrong thing. They try to solve a weight problem by jumping into a new fad diet without tackling the reasons why they overeat, or they move to the first new job that they can get and find themselves just as unhappy as before as they didn't take into account what they disliked about their old job and ended up in a similar role.

This is particularly true for you if you have picked this book up because you have a general sense that something isn't right in an area of your life but you aren't sure what it is or where to begin. Getting clear on what it is that you want to tackle is absolutely vital. Giving yourself the time and space now to think, analyse and get clear on what it is that you need to resolve, will mean that you can put your effort into the right things to give you the results that you want.

We start doing this by reviewing what you have written on your braindump list and digging down into each item in turn. This digging will allow us to get clear the specifics of what you need to resolve so we can start to develop action steps a little later on.

The best way I have found of doing this is to focus on uncovering the facts within your braindump that capture the actual impact that the problem is having on you. Taking an example from a consulting client of mine, he initially captured a thought that stated, "my job is extremely demanding". When he started to dig into how that demanding job impacted him, he reframed it and added "I am not able to switch off in the evenings", "I do not see my family as much as I would like", "I have to put in so many additional hours all I seem to do is work", "I can't look for an exit strategy as I don't have the time", "I feel trapped" onto his list. Being able to break his initial problem down further gave him a much clearer idea of the things he needed to work on.

If you have a lot of different problems or challenges on your mind, or even just one whopper with a few different strands, make sure you get clear on what each separate strand is at this stage. The most complex challenge I have undertaken recently was signing up for a charity trek to Everest Base Camp where not only did I have train for and complete the trek, I also had to raise a minimum of £9000 in sponsorship money at the same time.

Knowing that I was facing two distinct challenges - fundraising and physical readiness - made it easier for me to plan out how to tackle each one. Similarly, if your challenge is wanting to change your career, emigrate or start a new business you will find it easier to think about how these can start to break down into separate areas. Once you can identify these areas you can then break those down further and more easily plan out how to resolve the problem as a whole.

When you have completed a first pass of your braindump list, you may find it helpful to put your list away for a couple of days and come back to it with a fresh perspective for this next bit. The next stage is to go back through what you have previously written and run through a 3 Step Analysis:

1. Focus on impact

Make sure you have identified what makes this is a problem for you and not just what you think the solution is. As an example, if you have written "I need a new job", why do you feel that way? Do you dislike the environment, the company culture, the commute or the people you work with? If you can identify what is making you feel like that then you leave the door open to other solutions that may suit you better rather than being fixed on leaving your job as the only option. A good tool for this is to keep on asking "why?" after each reason you come up with and to keep drilling down 5 or 6 layers until you discover the real reason this is an issue. After analysis, you might find that your problem is more accurately described as "my relationship with a colleague isn't very good" and you are looking to escape from that by moving to a new job. Realising that this is the main reason gives you many more options for solving this problem.

2. Break it down

Break down one problem into smaller chunks if you need to in order to help you think clearly about each part of it. Make each of these chunks as small as you need to in order to gain clarity over what needs to be resolved. When I originally used this process to tackle my fixer-upper house, I broke "I want to sort my disaster of a house out" into a list of what needed to be done in each room. Having this lower level visibility made it much easier to see exactly what needed to be done.

3. Identify the root of the problem

Successfully delivering that new project at work, or shifting that final 2 stone in weight is the outcome you want to achieve but is not the root of the problem you are trying to overcome. In that first example, the underlying problem for the new project might be that no-one in your department has the right skills at the moment so that is what you need to focus on resolving to achieve the outcome. For the weight loss example, it might be that you exercise and diet brilliantly during the week but undo it all at the weekend as you can't resist beer and pizza evenings with your friends so to tackle that you need to focus on strategies to help manage weekend binges rather than just thinking about the weight loss you want.

Create a new list with the results of your analysis. We are going to call this the Problem List.

To illustrate how useful this 3 Step Analysis is, let me share an example of where I have used it to identify where a work project was focusing on the wrong thing. A warehousing company I worked with were introducing barcode scanners to the operation but were getting a lot of resistance from the workforce towards using them. The company had assumed that this resistance was due to the staff just being awkward and so had been trying to manage it accordingly with disciplinary action. My role was to train staff on their new working processes and how to use the scanners. During the first couple of training sessions with some of the staff it became apparent that the underlying reason for the resistance was fear from influential members of the shift teams around using the new "hi-tech" technology. Understanding that meant I could focus on finding ways to make the technology more familiar to them to reduce some of the fear they were feeling. What worked in this project was to introduce "laser-quest" style practicals to the training sessions, giving the staff a chance to play with the new scanners in a non-pressure setting which helped reduce both their fear of and resistance to the new technology.

One example of how I have used the above in my personal life was in overcoming the shyness that plagued my teens. How do you solve shyness? Quick answer is that you don't. Shyness is a concept and not something tangible but the impact it has on people is very real. In my case, I focused on the impact it was having on me i.e. the things it was stopping me from doing such as starting conversations with people I didn't know, making phonecalls, and going to places on my own. The underlying problems I found for each of these strands was very similar - I wasn't comfortable and so was worried about sounding stupid or getting something wrong, or drawing attention to myself in unfamiliar places. Taking the time to braindump my thoughts around this was fairly emotional at the time but helped me to identify that I needed to work on building my confidence in new situations and find ways to take the pressure off trying to create the "perfect" conversation. Armed with new clarity, I was able to implement strategies to extend my comfort zone and practice starting conversations so that I reduced the impact of my shyness on my day to day life.

If you find going back through your braindump list generates a lot of negative emotions which are difficult for you to get past, one technique that can help is taking a mental step back from the list and imagining that you are reviewing a friend's list instead as that can help introduce some objectivity. Overwhelm leads to inaction and all you will do is continue to spin on the spot with your thoughts unless you can break out of that cycle.

A client of mine got stuck in a loop at this point by being really fearful of taking on a new project at work. Fear magnifies any negative thoughts as you start to get caught in a downward spiral of "what if" if you don't take care to catch yourself. This client had managed to make a mental leap from having a new project to being homeless. She had followed a train of thought that project failing = job loss = no money = can't pay mortgage = living on the streets. In her head the problem was now not delivering a project but the whole survival of her way of life which left her unable to take any action through fear that she would do the wrong thing and end up ruined. She went through the braindump cycle several times over, destroying each version as she went along and leaving it a few days before repeating the cycle. This helped her to work off some of the emotion and get to the point where she could stop panicking and go through the 3-step analysis more objectively. If you are really struggling with this step then a similar approach may be useful for you to try too.

Wrap Up

Most people I work with find the braindump exercise a really freeing experience as everything is now out of their head and down on paper. I hope you have experienced the same feeling? When I first started to do this myself, it was that feeling of calm and the quieting of my internal chatter that kept me coming back to this exercise time after time. Eventually this became a habit, and even today, whenever I feel like I have something weighing on my mind, I reach for a pen and paper and get my thoughts out onto the page in front of me. I know that once I can articulate them I can dig into them. Once I dig into them I can get clear on what the core issue is then I can move forward and tackle it.

When you have completed this 3 Step Analysis process for yourself, join me in the next section where we will start to work with your Problem List.

2 SORTING

In this section we are going to take each one of the items you have captured on your Problem List, sort them into themes and prioritise them. We will then go a bit deeper into why you want to solve those problems and what solving them successfully would look like to you.

Sort the List

First up is sorting your list which in simple terms is grouping similar or related problems together. This step will help you to more easily identify potential projects that you can tackle. If you used some of the suggested categories in the braindump exercise (finances, career, home, family, friends and health) then these can also be useful as a guide here. Feel free to pick categories that resonate more with your situation but try not to use too many at this stage, 5-6 is plenty to start with and will stop things getting confused. When you are finished, each problem on your list should have an assigned category. If you are struggling to categorise one or more items, it may be that you need to revisit your 3 Step Analysis and clarify your wording, or even look at splitting that item into two or more smaller pieces that fit into different categories.

Set Priorities

Now you have created some groupings, select the category group that you want to work with first. If you aren't sure which one to start with, you could either pick the one that feels like a good starting point for you, or sometimes the easiest place is the category that contains the most problems! Once you have selected a category, you are now going to go through the items in it and start to prioritise the ones that are the most important for you. When you have a number of things that you want to fix, it is really easy to get over-enthusiastic and try and do them all at once, however, humans really do not multi-task very well at all (despite a lot of today's "life hack gurus" trying to tell you otherwise). It is far more effective to focus on one important thing and move that forward than it is jumping from task to task to task and not really progressing anything. Taking the time to prioritise properly will allow you to be confident that you are focused on fixing those things that will have the most positive impact for you first.

I find that a simple 1-5 numbering system has

always worked for me when prioritising - 1 being the highest priority and 5 being the lowest. There are two key drivers you need to consider when assigning a rating to each of the items on your list: urgency and importance. If something is urgent that usually means that it is time-sensitive and if you are under stress, urgent problems can give a sense of needing to be done now or the world will end. In contrast, if something is important it has the potential to have a much greater impact on your life, but if you are not careful, the progress of important tasks can often be 'parked' while your attention is focused on tackling a succession of urgent (but less important) things. Identifying which problems are important rather than just urgent will ensure you tackle the ones that will be of most benefit to you in the long run. Please take the time to think about these priorities carefully and assign your ratings accordingly.

The aim with prioritisation is to only give yourself a handful of things to work on at once. This will enable you to focus on a couple of key things and make real progress. Now look at the priority ratings you have assigned. Those items with high ratings (1 or 2) are the ones you should look to action first. Let's start calling these your Action List. The medium and low ratings (3 to 5) you can park for the moment and review again after you have dealt with the high priority ones. If your Action List contains more than 3-4 items at this stage, you will need to review the prioritisation that you have just done and really focus on finding those 3-4 things that are the most important to do first. Your list isn't going anywhere and you can always come back to the other things later.

Push and Pull

As you are working through your Action List, you will notice that you are drawn to things you want to do (pull) and are trying to avoid other things (push).

Things you feel a pull towards could be dreams you have always had but not yet acted upon. Maybe a closet dream of yours has always to have been a writer but you have never really given it much thought or pursued it at all as you feel that kind of career path is for the special chosen few and not for "people like you". Or maybe you would really love to help other people overcome their health and fitness challenges but can't see that ever happening as you are currently overweight and unfit yourself.

In either of these scenarios if this being possible for you is something you can't get your head around right now then that is absolutely fine. Keep that secret dream in your head and set yourself a "next step" destination on your internal Satnav that you can see yourself being able to achieve. Maybe move into a role that is less demanding so you have the energy to try your hand at writing for a bit in the evenings, or maybe set your target weight and a fitness target and then go and join a club/class where you can start supporting other people and share your journey on social media to inspire others. When you start to align even small choices with that bigger picture, you will start to change how you think about yourself and that will help you to refine that end destination more and more.   You can keep setting "next step" destinations as often as you need to and adjust them as needed once your direction becomes clearer.

If you simply can't see that far ahead from where you are now, then let's take a look at the other end of the scale. What negative impact are the high priority items on your list having on your life right now? Are they causing you stress, if so what about? Are they stopping you doing other things, if so what kinds of things and how do you feel about that? Or to put it another way, what is it that you want to stop?   Get as specific as you can manage at the moment on these. When I created my first list my house was one of my top priority problems. I was so far away from being able to visualise my "dream home" at that time as I was living in a disaster zone! All I wanted was for the chaos to stop, for things to work as they should (our hot water had recently become a fetching shade of orange as the immersion tank had corroded), and to be able to have guests over without having to spend an hour moving things out of the way so they had somewhere to sit. Those are what I pinned my emotional connection to so I could use that emotion to motivate me. This may take a little time for you to explore but it is well worth it for the clarity you will gain.

Starting to take action without being clear on why and you may find that you either lose focus on resolving your problem, or you will resolve it and realise it hasn't made the difference you thought it would. Once you have tapped into the real "why" behind your wish to solve this problem you will find your inner strength to actually achieve it.

For example, perhaps one of the items on your Problem List is that you want to lose weight. You may think your "why" is quite obvious at first (for example to look good in swimwear for an upcoming beach holiday) but as you take the time to think around this more deeply, you may find that the real "why" is because you want to feel that you respect your health and your body which will, in turn, fuel your self-confidence. Or you may find your "why" is making sure your kids don't grow up with a weight problem so that you want to lead by example. Once you have that "why" nailed you can use it to for clarity and support if you start to waver from your action plan later. Reminding yourself as you reach for that snack that you want to reach your ideal weight so that your kids copy your example will help to keep you on track.

Using your Satnav

When you are putting time, energy and effort into

resolving your problem you need to know that there is a specific end point where you can say "The End" and call the problem solved. I like using a Satnav analogy at this point with "The End" being the destination I enter. The journey to that destination starts to become my "project" once I am clear on where I want to go. A project has a defined outcome and a defined timescale within which to achieve that outcome. Starting to think in terms of "your project" rather than "your problem" can help you to take the first steps towards thinking about the practicalities of how you will solve it - setting an outcome for you to achieve and setting a target deadline. Most people without a deadline to work to will turn into masters of procrastination, locked into a cycle of promising themselves that they will start on Monday - and we all know how well that works!

How do you decide what target deadline to set and what success looks like for you? This is something that you need to work out for yourself. There is no right or wrong answer here. For most people this runs a fine line between pushing themselves and being too safe. If this is something you are new to doing then picking something safe is absolutely fine to start with, just make sure you get crystal clear on what you are counting as success from your reachable target so you don't beat yourself up with "shoulds" when you have reached your goal. You could choose to do something with a set target built in like a sponsored run or like my Everest Base

Camp challenge to raise £9k in 9 months, or you can set your own deadlines like deciding you want a new job by Christmas. Other things might be more subjective and require a bit more exploration in terms of setting the target that is right for you, such as lose weight, make new friends, not feel stressed. If you don't know where to start with this, I would suggest the following exercise to get you thinking.

Pick any one of the items on your action list and write what you would like to see for these 3 things:

1. The ideal result,

2. The smallest result you would settle for,

3. A result in between 1 and 2 that you would be happy with,

Certainly, when I first started doing this, the targets I ended up setting for myself were hovering between 2 and 3 and to be honest I wasn't always sure I could even make 2! But as I started to achieve little wins and achieve all my 2s, I started to trust myself and found it easier to start aiming for some 1s as that usually guaranteed I would hit my 3s.

Knowing where you are heading to is a great start but planning a route to Edinburgh is very different depending on whether your starting point is Glasgow or Albuquerque. Your Satnav needs to know where you are right now. Personally, I don't spend a lot of time exploring or analysing the "now" as I found that a lot of what I discovered ended up being irrelevant. I have also seen this with coaching clients who have spent years over-analysing how and why they got to where they are now and they ended up just stuck circling around the same things rather than taking the action needed to make a change. What has been much more effective is to identify what "right" looks like for the issue you are trying to resolve and then mobilise the necessary resources to get there.

There are a number of ways to capture where you are now but I would encourage you to focus on what can either be directly measured, or using something that can be turned into actual data-points. The most common way of measuring something is counting down towards your target. For example, if your goal is weight loss - tracking pounds or kilos lost and how many are left until you reach your target is one direct measurement. Business processes also lend themselves well to this sort of measurement as there is usually a time/cost metric in there somewhere.

If your objective is something less tangible, such as to feel healthier, you could think about tracking data like hours of sleep, or number of balanced meals eaten. Another approach for tracking intangible objectives is to define your own measurement criteria. You can use the classic 1-5 scale again and assign a starting value to what you want to track and use that as a base measurement to track

> "People do two things: what
> they want to do and what
> they are measured on, and
> that's it."
> **Phil M Jones**

progress against. Where you have intangible things that you feel are important to track, record how you would currently rate your health/relationships/fitness/stress levels etc. Once you have the values set down as they are today, you can track progress against them over time and see how your plan is working for you.

Now your journey has a start and an end point, your Satnav can not only plan the route ahead, but also so you can now also see how far you have come and how far you have left to go. We will talk more about measuring progress later on. What is important at this stage is to understand and make note of your starting level as a basis for tracking your progress. I don't know about you, but I always used to move the goalposts on myself when I started something new. Actually, I can find myself edging towards doing this sometimes even now! What I have found is if I don't take the time to clearly capture where I am starting from, I will continually move my target further away as I am working through my project. This delivers the double whammy of knocking my motivation (I am doing all this work and not getting anywhere) and my confidence (I still can't do/am no good at/haven't completed xyz).

One recent example I can share from my own life is that I created myself a project to write this book, but I gave no consideration when I started to either what I thought success would look like, or the fact I hadn't written anything since high school and I was now in my early 40s! In the end I wrote a 40000 word book that I should have been instantly proud of, but once I had completed it my brain decided to present me with a long list of things that I *should* have written instead. It had taken me several months of hard work, but I now felt like I had failed. I didn't give myself credit for the work I had done, just decided that it wasn't enough after I changed my own goalposts and I almost parked the whole thing. What changed that viewpoint for me was reminding myself of the note I had made of my starting point (i.e. zero books written before!) which helped me to keep my achievement in perspective.

Once you have identified your why and set target outcomes for each of the high priority items on your Action List, let's move on and put the final pieces in place so we can start to put your action plan together.

3 DETANGLING

Sometimes I can fly through the steps in the last section - see what I want to do, work out a target, set my starting point and then I am ready to start working out how to get there. Other times I can really struggle with parts of (or even all of!) that process as there are some other internal issues holding me back. This section deals with the three main things that I have found can hold me back and have also been holding back some of my clients.

A note on what YOU want

Getting clear on why you want to resolve the problems you listed is important. This knowledge will give you the internal motivation you need to keep going if you hit a roadblock later down the line. Internal is the key word in that last sentence. There is a really important distinction to be made here, you need to be very, very clear on what it is that YOU want. Not what your partner wants, not what your friend wants for you, not what you think you should do, not what you have read that's the latest "recipe for success". All of these other reasons will result in failure because your heart isn't really in it. In my experience, if I am trying to motivate myself to do something, unless I have an emotional connection to what I am trying to do, I will simply not do it.

Spend some time asking yourself what it is that you want to get out of solving these problems in your life. Our culture of "bigger, brighter, faster" tends to suggest that the only valid goals are ones that take you as high as possible - aim to be champion of the world or don't bother as it doesn't count. Figuring some of this out kept me stuck in a few areas of my life for ages as I allowed myself to be swayed by other people's opinions rather than thinking about what I wanted.

On one memorable occasion I had decided I was going to take up running to get fit, so I booked myself onto a 5k Race for Life and raise money for charity whilst I was at it. On sharing this with colleagues in the office, there was one person who clearly thought this wasn't good enough and decided to share his opinion with me. I should have booked myself into a marathon as 5k is too easy, my target time of sub 35 minutes was ridiculous as Mo Farah could run it in less than half that time so I should push myself, a sponsorship target of £100 was too low and no incentive at all, etc. I am sure you have met someone similar! My first response to this was to think about changing my plans after all he was an experienced runner so must be worth listening to? Instead I reconnected with why I wanted to do the run and my reasons were to get fit, have some accountability through sponsorship, and prove to myself that I could run 5k (which seemed an enormous distance when I struggled to run for more than 30 seconds at time). This 5k Race for Life was meeting all the criteria for what I wanted to do so I stuck with it and ignored my colleague's input.

It is important to be authentic to yourself and not just follow what you think you "should" be doing. Picking up on the Satnav analogy - you are the one in control of what goes into your Satnav - only you can set your destination, so make sure you think about what you want and what would make you happy.

Self-imposed Limits

One challenge people have is how to overcome or see past the limits they set on themselves. As described brilliantly in Carol Dweck's book Mindset, a lot of people have a fixed view of who they are, what they are capable of and therefore what they think is possible for them to achieve. Many people will approach new things by saying "I can't see myself doing that". The perception of who they are versus what they see another person doing is too great a leap for how they see themselves, they therefore discount it immediately as an option to pursue.

I had a colleague a few years ago whose dream was to ditch the corporate lifestyle in favour of creating artisan metalwork for a living. She was really talented and already made things for her home and as gifts for friends, but she just could not see herself as an artist after 20 years as a spreadsheet warrior in an office. She decided to stay put and gave up on her dream. I often wonder what happened to her. In my own life for many years I struggled with the concept of calling myself "creative". As an example from my own life, I have always been really good at solving problems and am reasonably ok at other artistic things (enough to keep myself happy anyway!) but if I ever started to look at making more of one of those creative talents I would always tell myself "I am not creative" - my self-image was very much biased towards my analytical skills. I held similar limiting beliefs around how far "someone like me" could go in my career, what my body was and wasn't capable of doing, and how my life would pan out.

Over the years I have wrestled with my mindset on various subjects on many occasions, and still do from time to time. Setting targets was always difficult for me. Answering questions like "Where do you see yourself in 10 years' time?" was always a challenge as I always tried to answer those

> "May your choices
> reflect your hopes, not
> your fears."
> Nelson Mandela

truthfully, and the truth is for many years I had no idea!

How I worked around this was to keep a vague sense of direction in mind but focus only on what I wanted my immediate next step to be. Just going for the next step reduced the scale of change I was trying to make into something that felt manageable. Instead of feeling pressured into looking for something to do for the rest of my life, I was instead looking at what was possible for me to do right now. After doing this a few times I became more comfortable with taking bigger steps and starting to sketch out a longer-term view of where I was aiming for.

In the last couple of years I have been able to push myself a lot further but it took hiring my own coach to really enable me to do that. It can be hard to take that really good look at yourself and see past current you to what new you could achieve but it is so worth it in the end. Once I clicked around what was possible for me, it was like a whole new world had opened up.

Dealing with Fear

Fear is one of the most powerful emotions we possess as humans. You will soon realise that fear is always going to be a part of your journey and that through fear you will try your best to stop yourself reaching your goals, particularly if there is a large degree of personal change needed to get you there. Fear has the ability to derail you at any point along your journey and it will attempt to sabotage you in a number of different ways, most commonly as fear of failure and fear of success.

Fear of failure is the one that is most likely to stop us from doing the things that we want to do. A key part of fear of failure is fear of looking stupid in front of others and tackling this is the reason that we spent time getting crystal clear on what your specific goal was around your specific problem. Locking that down at the start and keeping that in mind will really help you stop self-sabotaging before you even start what you are trying to do.   To illustrate what I mean about how fear can derail you, how many times have you said something like "this time I will really stick to my diet", or "that's me now only drinking at weekends", or "I'm going to go for a run every morning before work" and also been aware that you've added a mental footnote in to the tune of (let's see how long this lasts this time)? You are already setting yourself up for failure due to lack of belief that you can achieve the goal. This lack of belief is not a reflection on your capability, rather you are using this as a protection mechanism - avoiding sticking your neck out as if you do stumble then it means you can always tell yourself that you always knew it wouldn't work anyway.

Fear of success operates in a similar way. It may seem counter-intuitive to harbour fears about actually achieving your goal but what you are really doing here is worrying about the unknown and how you will need to go through personal change to achieve your goal. As an example, imagine the current version of you visits the gym 3 times a week for a couple of months. You make great progress and are really enjoying it but then your thoughts start to wander and you start to question whether you are cut out to be one of those marathon-running/weight-lifting super fit people you see around the gym. Maybe thinking that you might be one of them in a few months is worrying as you have no idea what that will mean for current you. The current you may be a bit squishier than you would like to be but when you are thinner and fitter, what if you are no longer the same person? What if your whole outlook on food and exercise change? What if you stop wanting to order that Friday night curry with your partner? What if your relationship suffers? You will find a whole load of "what ifs" creeping into your thoughts and they can get really scary.

To stop that internal chatter, you resist becoming that person. You find excuses not to go to the gym and stay as you were. In a similar vein, looking at making a career change can introduce similar thought paths. What if you make the wrong decision about moving? What if the new career is worse than the one you are currently in? What if you don't like the new company? What if you don't make friends with your new colleagues? What if you can't handle the new job you have taken and your professional reputation is ruined?

Getting caught into a cycle of "what if" happens to everyone at some point. The best way I have found of getting out of the tailspin when it happens to me is to revisit some of the earlier steps in this process and write all the what ifs down so they are not just swirling around in my head. I then review each one and validate that against my goal to gain some perspective. This helps me acknowledge the fear that I have but also carry on working towards my goal.

It is important to recognise that as you work towards a goal and look to improve an aspect of your life, you will change in some way by doing so. New skills, new experiences, new outlooks all come with the territory. You need to be prepared to accept that the current you will change and that this may have some impact on relationships that you have outgrown. Some people never spend the time thinking about what they want to do or taking action towards their goals as they are so paralysed by fear of change that they try and remain the same as they have always been. Do you want to be like those people, or do you want to do the things you are capable of and embrace the personal change needed to achieve that? You need to make a choice.

4 EXPLORING

Now it is time to start thinking about how you are going to get to the outcome you want. I will show you the exact methods I have used for many years to break down and manage projects and I will also show you how to explore different options for achieving your goal and establish which ones are right for you to take forward. Once you have been through this exercise you will be able to define what specific and measurable actions you will need to undertake to get you to your destination. Remember, you cannot successfully deliver on just a concept.

The first step is to re-write your Action List as a series of questions that align with the target outcome you have set yourself. The reason for using questions is that questions invite answers - you will automatically start to think of ways to answer the question. Those answers will, in turn, give you options to consider. If we take an example, instead of a statement like "I need a new job" that you may have started with, you may re-frame it as a question like this: "What do I need to do to in the next 6 months to get a new job that pays £50000pa, allows me to travel and allows me to use my creative skills to help customers as those are the things that are important to me". Can you see this immediately invites looking for a solution?

Some more examples for how to change your problem statements into questions are as follows:

- I need to lose weight = What do I need to do to get to my target weight of 140lbs by Christmas?

- I need to make more money = What do I need to do to raise my income by £5000 this year?

- I want to change careers = What do I need to do to enable me to gain skills to help this happen?

Once you have your list of questions, we need to start getting some answers to work with. To help you do this, I will be stepping you through some real-life examples from clients of mine to illustrate how they have used this method. The first example is fairly straightforward so you can see how the process works for a very specific project. Further examples show how the same technique can be used for projects that are a bit more open-ended; in one case the client is on a journey to identify a new direction in their life.

Mind Maps

The technique I want to show you here is called Mind Mapping. Mind Mapping is really useful in helping you think around a particular problem, identify elements that need to be considered and to start to think about possible solutions. I use this all the time, both at home and at work, as seeing it laid out in front of me really does help me think. This is a very visual technique and is great for helping you see various elements of a potential solution and how they interact. If you have not come across Mind Maps before, they are really simple to create!

The steps are as follows:

1. Pick a key word that you want to generate ideas around.

2. Draw a circle in the centre of a piece of paper.

3. Write your key word inside the circle

4. Think about one idea that you have related to that key word

5. Draw another circle and write that idea into it.

6. Draw a line linking the new circle to the

centre circle.

7. Repeat until you run out of ideas around your key word.

8. Pick one of your ideas and think about any other ideas that spark for you.

9. Put those into a circle and link them back to the idea.

10. Repeat for as many times as you want.

This cycle of thinking of ideas related to other ideas can continue for as many levels as you think are required to fully explore and brainstorm your question. The end result can be fairly simple like the first example, or more complex depending on how much depth you go into. Take a look at the examples below, then have a go at this yourself.

<u>Example 1</u>:

What do I need to do to fund raise £9000 for my charity trek? I currently have zero pounds and 9 months in which to raise it all.

My starting point with this was to put the framework of the plan together. Raising £9000 off the bat was quite a daunting target and I didn't want to get trapped into a mindset of being over-awed by the amount. The obvious thing for me to do with this one was to split it down so there was a target to raise £1000 per month instead. This was still going to be a stretch but for me, raising £1000 and repeating that 9 times felt a lot more manageable. Having those nine £1000 interim targets also gave me a really good metric to track my progress against.

My next step was to think about how I could make £1000. This is where the Mind Mapping technique was really useful. I came up with 3 initial ideas - selling, sponsorship and events, and I brainstormed around each of those. The map I created for the fundraising challenge looked roughly like this:

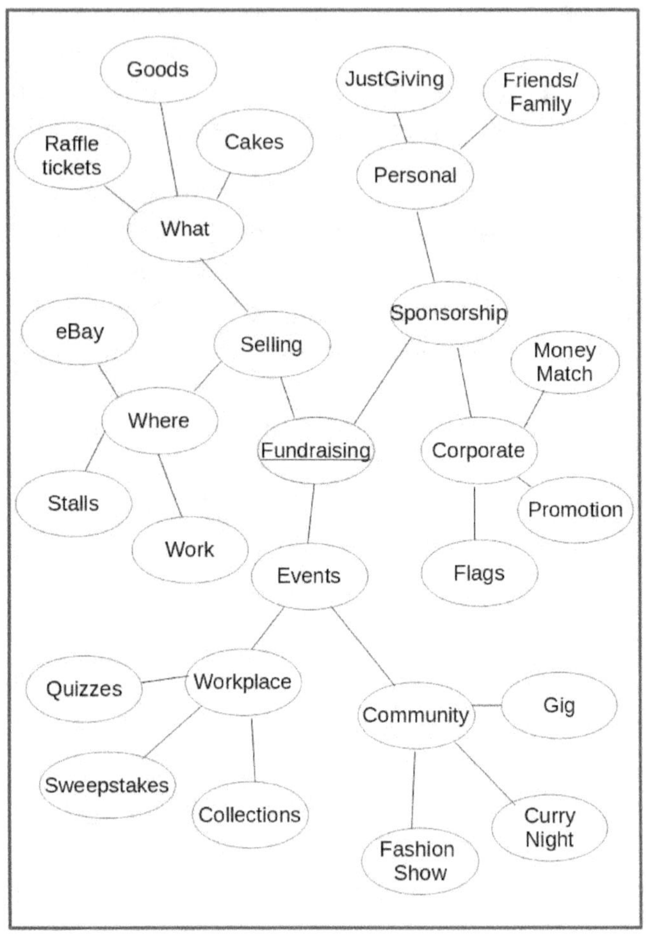

I took each arm of the diagram and worked through each of them in more detail adding more notes and ideas as I went. Having it all laid out on a page like this for me, meant I could easily see which ones might be quick wins, which might be less feasible and which ones I might need to research a bit more. If you find that one of your circles is generating a lot of questions, you might find it useful to break that one out into its own separate Mind Map and drill down further. The aim is to get a question that is specific enough to answer behind each circle, such as:

- How much could I make out of a cake sale?

- How many sales could I realistically fit into 9 months?

- What other goods could I sell?

- Do I have any spare things at home I could sell on eBay?

- Can I make other things and sell them?

- Could I find other goods to resell and use the profit for the fund?

- How would I find opportunities for free/low cost start-up opportunities to sell goods?

- Where can I find donations for raffle prizes?

- Is there a suitable venue locally for a fundraising gig?

- Is there a suitable restaurant I could contact to discuss a curry night?

- What are the conditions around my company's money match scheme?

- Can I find local businesses who might want to sponsor me?

- What's the best way of promoting the trek to reach more people to sponsor me?

I think you get the idea! What I was left with at the end of the session on this was a list of ideas and activities I could explore further and work with to start to formulate a plan to meet my target of raising £9000 in 9 months.

Let's now take a look at how that same process can be used to tackle other topics.

Example 2:

This next example is based on a client of mine with some details changed to preserve their anonymity. Let's call this person Sam. Sam started working life straight out of university in a technical job directly related to his degree. He'd had a strong interest in the subject matter at school so it seemed like as good a choice as any for a career.

15 years down the line however, Sam was struggling. He was outwardly successful - married, 2 kids, nice car, surplus income, senior position at work, but he wasn't happy. He felt like he was treading water, lacking the enthusiasm he had once

had for his career, unable to see himself doing the same thing for the next 20 years but having no clue what to do next. He got in touch with me as he wanted to explore what his options might be for making a change.

Having gone through the exercises in the previous section and exploring what he really liked doing and what his ideal future career would look like, Sam rediscovered a passion for helping people.

He used to spend time at university volunteering by helping adults develop basic IT skills and early in his career, he was part of a large team of new recruits with varying specialisms so he was heavily involved in cross-training efforts with his colleagues. Sam also had time to volunteer on the staff social committee and organised a number of staff events which he really enjoyed.

Fast forward a few years and Sam found that taking on additional responsibilities and moving up the ladder crowded out those kinds of interactions and time to participate in the "extra-curricular" activities. He still enjoyed part of his job, however, in his current role, he felt that the work he did primarily benefited the corporation but did little to benefit the people he worked with.

He had begun to feel really disconnected and isolated from the other people at his company and had started to feel like he was really in the wrong place. Sam's main question was: "What do I need to do to spend more of my time working to help and support real people?"

Sam's Mind Map looked like this:

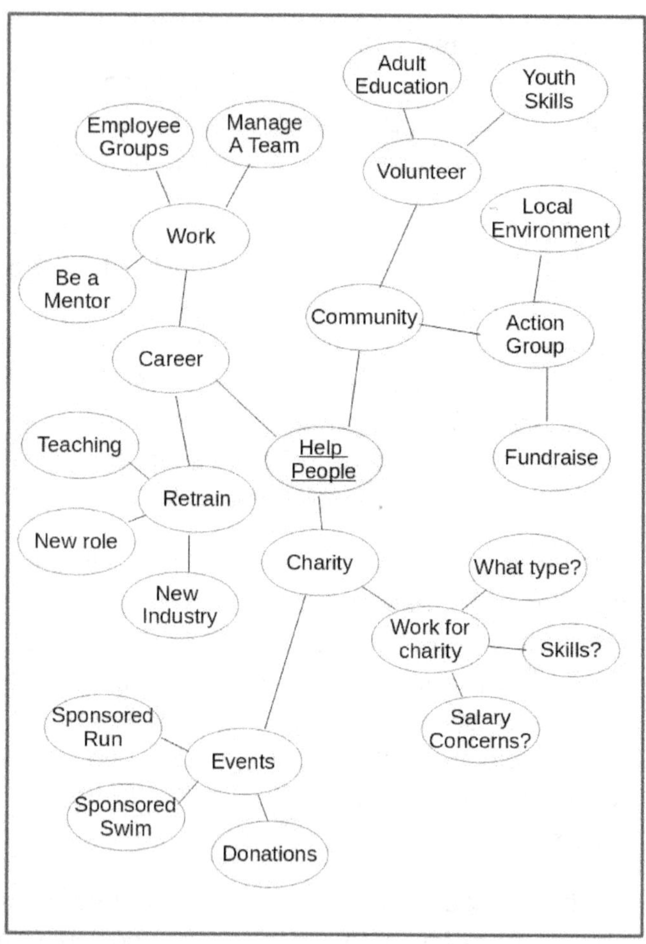

This gave Sam a few options to explore and to think about how he felt about them. He liked the idea of doing more for charity and volunteering and the exercise had brought up things he hadn't really thought about properly before, like adapting parts of his current role.   He liked the idea of team management and mentoring rather than retraining and having a fresh start in a new industry.

<u>Example 3:</u>

Jo was another client of mine who was making a case for a promotion where she worked. She knew that she needed to make a success of a project she had been given following a merger by her company.

Jo is an office manager who, with her small team of administrators, is going to be responsible for a lot more work than she was before.   She isn't automatically going to get any additional staff to enable this as her management chain expect her to fit as much of the extra workload in as possible and then take a reading on whether additional team members are actually needed. She has 3 months before the first of the new work is expected to come in to prepare her assessment and prepare her team.

Again, Jo has been through the exercises in the first part of this book. Her "What do I need to do" question is "What do I need to do to deliver the additional work required of my team in 3 months' time"

Jo's mind map looks like this:

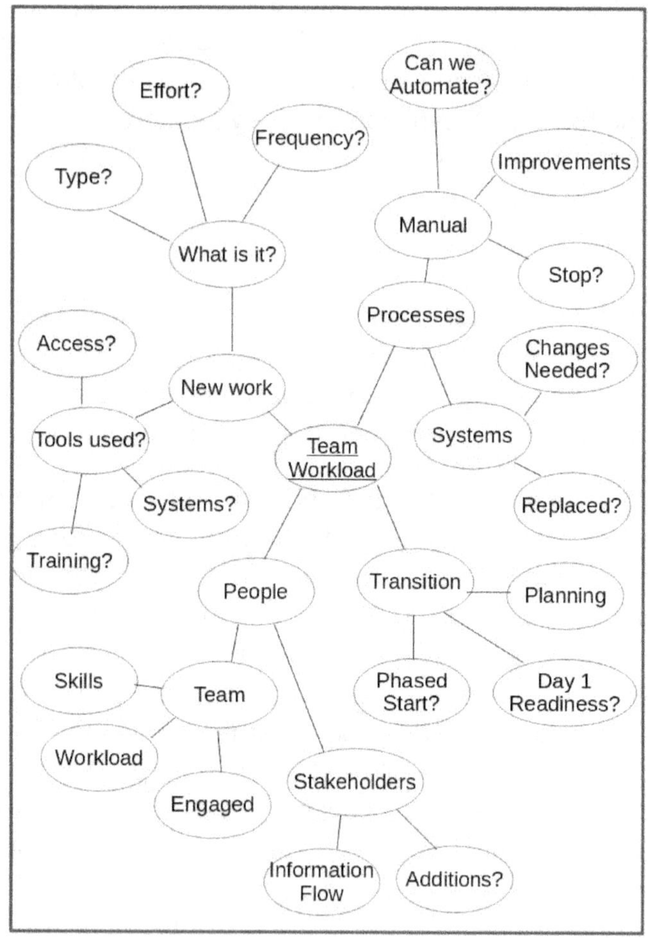

This helped Jo identify some of the things she needs to think about plus highlight topics that she needs to go and research before she can really begin planning. Jo has indicated those areas with a question mark on her map and will add tasks around information gathering into her planning as she doesn't currently know enough about the new work coming in to be able to plan to take it on successfully.

Jo can also see from the questions on her map that there are a number of different areas that will potentially need new tools or processes to be implemented and so she is unlikely to have time to do all of this work herself and she will need to engage her existing team to help her. Her immediate action from the Mind Mapping exercise is to approach her team and get them onboard with the project.

In all three of the examples in this section, high level activities, questions and ideas to explore are clearer now than they were before the Mind Mapping exercise. I knew what my next steps were, as did Sam and Jo. Have a go now at creating your own Mind Map. Once you have done that, answer the following questions:

1. What are the immediate things you have learned from it?

2. What immediate action steps could you take?

3. Where do you need more information?

4. Did it bring up anything unexpected?

5. How can you use the answers to the previous questions to further enhance your map?

Let's go and build you an action plan!

End of Section Checklist

You have prioritised what you want to look at first.

You have identified the specific problem you need to solve

You have asked yourself the right questions to help you solve it.

You have created some options to explore.

Part Two

CREATE A PLAN

5 CHOICES

In this section we are going to work out what you need to be focusing on first, and working out the right level of task to allow you to take action. Once we have this clear, in the next section we will work on putting them into the right order and creating a plan, but before we get to that, we need to start with the information in your Mind Maps and analyse the options you came up with in order to determine two things:

1. Which option you want to explore first,

2. What your starting point will be.

Which option are you going to pick first?

I used to find this question really tough to answer. I would look at all the paths I could now take and found myself overwhelmed by choice and effectively paralysed. Worrying that although I know I need to pick somewhere to start, what if I pick the wrong thing to do first? What if I spend lots of time and effort going in one direction and then find that another direction would have been better? Does this sound familiar?

I think we have all been there at some point. The truth is that unless you are blessed with the gift of foresight, you are never going to know 100% if you have made the right choice before you start. The best way I have found to deal with this is to actually make a start. Pick something and do it.

If you do start off following one path and then decide later that actually another path is a better fit for what you want to achieve then by all means you can switch the new path instead. You haven't wasted time with a false-start, you have instead built up some additional knowledge and experience that you can call on later.

If you stay stuck in indecision and fail to make a start at all then not only have you not made any progress, you also haven't learnt anything from it. You are simply the same as you were before but with time passing you by.

To make the decision-making easier for me, I always take a little time to weigh up each option that I could take so I can add some objectivity around which one looks most sensible to start with. Sometimes I go with the sensible choice, sometimes I go with gut feel but I have at least considered the merits of each option. Using the prioritisation techniques from earlier in the book for each option is a good starting point.

Another simple technique I use is to create a list of 'for' and 'against' for each option. I like to add a bit of a twist to this - I add not only for and against each option but also what I expect to happen if I do it, and what will happen if I don't. This allows me to identify areas that could lead to the greatest success for me, or those that create the biggest negative if I don't do them.

I have included an example here from my fundraising project which, if you remember from the Mind Map, brought forward three options: selling, sponsorship and events. I split the sponsorship and events categories down a little as you can see below, and my quick analysis worked out as follows:

<u>Selling:-</u>

FOR:	AGAINST:
Contacts already for things I can sell. Easy to start.	Only making margin so will need to move volume. Labour intensive.
IF I DO: Will get me off the mark quickly with some cash. Raise awareness of my cause.	IF I DON'T: Introduces more pressure into other areas to make money which would be less within my control.

<u>Sponsorship (Corporate):-</u>

FOR:	AGAINST:
Potential to get several hundred pounds in one go.	Time consuming to identify which companies to approach. May work better last-minute?
IF I DO: Will eat chunks of my target and could lead to referrals for more sponsors.	IF I DON'T: If I don't ask I won't get. If no takers then will have to work harder in other areas.

Sponsorship (Personal):-

FOR:	AGAINST:
Easy to set up and could get immediate donations, Effective final rally to the target.	Asking too early may lead to reduced donations. People annoyed with repeat requests?
IF I DO:	IF I DON'T:
Top up to meet the target; Raise awareness and gain supporters.	Not asking would penalise people who want to help, Reduces ability to raise awareness.

Events (small):-

FOR:	AGAINST:
Cheap and easy to organise. Can staff it myself.	Limited earning potential. Will need to do several repeat events.
IF I DO:	IF I DON'T:
Continual awareness of my fundraising, Opening up more potential personal donors;	Adds more pressure to the other options..

<u>Events (large):</u>-

<table>
<tr><td>FOR:

One large event could make more than half my target.</td><td>AGAINST:

Initial financial outlay required.
Added risk to find attraction and sell enough tickets.</td></tr>
<tr><td>IF I DO:
Good exposure for the fundraising.

Further collecting opportunities on the day.</td><td>IF I DON'T:

Financial risk for large event is avoided,

More work required on the other options..</td></tr>
</table>

I didn't spend more than a few minutes jotting down my thoughts around each option. Seeing this small piece of analysis on paper enabled me to make an informed choice about what areas I could start working with immediately - for me this was the selling and the small events categories. The other areas I decided to put to one side for the moment they required further research before I would be in a position to take anything forward with them.

Knowing the order in which to tackle the options you have is a key part of formulating your plan so we will come back to this later on.

Before then, let's go back to Sam and see how this same process applies to a few examples from his Mind Map around finding ways to support people.

For Sam the end game he wants to achieve is not as clear-cut as my fundraising example above. Sam knows roughly where he would like to go but there are still a few areas that he wants to explore around how he can support other people before he commits to a firm end goal. Sam's quick analysis around his career options look like this:

<u>Career change:-</u>

FOR: Easy to discuss with my manager. Will gain clarity on whether I need to move to a new company.	AGAINST: Many variables. I still have no clear direction. Need to explore more options before I action.
IF I DO: Would enable me to be much more fulfilled at work.	IF I DON'T: I will have no better insight into my options and may be stuck for further planning..

Whilst his volunteering options look like this:

<u>Volunteering:-</u>

<table>
<tr><td>FOR:

Will help me to immediately feel like I am helping people.</td><td>AGAINST:

Time invested in volunteering may slow down progress in the other areas.</td></tr>
<tr><td>IF I DO:
Creating more connections and building experience that could facilitate a career change.</td><td>IF I DON'T:

May miss out on valuable experience and new connections...</td></tr>
</table>

After repeating the same process with all the areas of his Mind map he wanted to explore, Sam observed that there were some immediate steps that he could take. Signing up for a sponsored charity event and setting up a career conversation with his manager were things he could do quite quickly, whereas the other items that would have a greater impact on his current lifestyle would need more time to consider fully.

Taking time to explore this has given Sam enough information to develop a starting point for a timeline as he knows which options he wants to look at first and which he wants to push to later on.

Go ahead and do the same for your options now. What can you start to action fairly quickly? What needs to be done later?

What's your starting point?

To help us in the next section, let's spend a bit of time now thinking about how we can fit your options onto a rough timeline. From your previous analysis, you will have identified some areas you can take action on quite quickly and some areas that will need to be parked for the moment to come back to later. Now you know these two things, you can start to create a really high-level timeline within which you can develop your action plan.

You may be asking why you need to develop a timeline at all? If you are anything like me, I'll bet that unless there is some sort of deadline attached to the things you want to do, it is very easy to just not do anything at all! I can be a world-class procrastinator if I give myself the wiggle room to push things back until later. I'll cover more about dealing with procrastination in a later section but suffice it to say I have never seen anything be completed in terms of personal projects or business projects that had a deadline of "someday" attached to it. If you don't have an external deadline imposed on what you are doing, you need to give yourself one to work to or you are setting yourself up for failure from the outset.

To start putting your timeline together, take the

immediate action steps that you identified from your Mind Map analysis and plot out when you think you could get those done by - next week, within a month? There often isn't an exact science to this and initial plans are often a best guess with the information known at the time. I always start with a basic high-level timeline as a plan for my project and then build it out in more detail as I go along, adjusting timings as necessary.

For my fundraising project, I had definitely decided on running some small event sales (table top sales in this case) and also knew I wanted to research some other options. I had 9 months in which to fundraise so I decided that holding 4 of them would be realistic - one every 2 months. I drew a simple timeline out for the 9 months and marked off a sale in months 2, 4, 6 and 8.

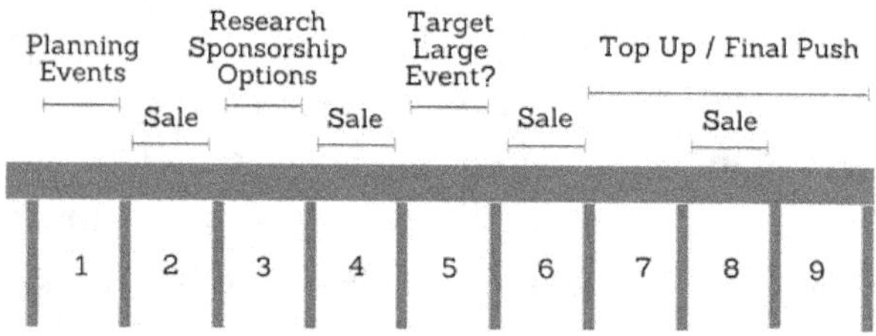

Month 1 I marked up as "planning events" to give me some time to find events, book a table and decide on what to sell at each.

Month 3 I marked up as "research sponsorship options", month 5 as "target large event?" and months 7 to 9 as "Top up/final push". This gave me enough of a framework to work with in more detail.

Back to Sam's example, Sam drew up a timeline covering an initial 4 month period. He decided that he could realistically tackle the first 2 things on his list - signing up for a sponsored charity event and setting up a career conversation with his manager - within the next few weeks so he put those into month 1 of his timeline.

Investigating options within his local community for volunteering around skills development in adults or young people, would take a bit more thought but he could start looking at options around that in month 2. Sam also knew that realistically any follow ups to his career conversations at work would take a while to move through the corporate machine so he marked month 3 as time to focus on progressing those. Month 4 he plotted out for review time to check on what progress he had been able to make.

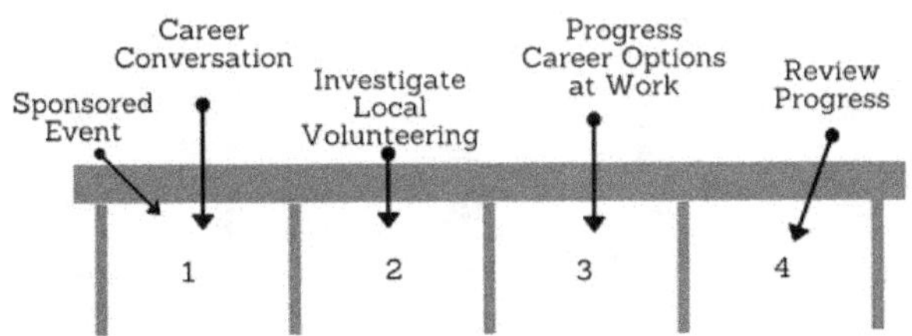

You may be wondering why Sam spaced these things as he did and why he didn't try and start them all at the same time or start them closer together? Sam felt that the timeline he chose gave enough gap between the activities to be able to focus properly on each one rather than try and stack up so much at the front end of the plan that he overwhelmed himself with trying to juggle too much too soon.

The next step is to take that high-level timeline and break down the activities within your action areas so that you have individual tasks to slot in to your plan. I will talk you through how to do this in the next section.

6 TASKS

One problem that I see tripping people up time and again is that they try to take action on something that is just too big to tackle in one go. They then either get caught out by problems they had not anticipated, or realise that as it was a much bigger job than they had first thought. This means they will struggle to get it all done in the time allotted and fall behind on their plan. The way to avoid this is to break down what you are trying to do into much smaller chunks. In simple terms, these chunks ideally need to be at the "one chunk = one action" level. I am going to refer to these 'one action chunks' as Tasks as we move forward in this section.

You may be asking why is it so important to get the right level of task identified? You know what you need to achieve overall so why do you need to bother breaking this down further? To illustrate why you really shouldn't skip this step, let's take one of Sam's outputs from the last section: to sign up for a sponsored charity event. That sounds like a simple enough thing to do so would count as one task, right? However, if you really think it through, there are a few things that Sam needs to either do or know before he can actually complete this action. He would need to decide on which charity he felt strongly about supporting, what type of event he wanted to do - run, swim, cycle, walk - does he want to do something locally or is he happy to travel further afield? Then he would need to decide what level of minimum sponsorship he could commit to, when he would like to do the event (based on how much training he might need to do, what other commitments he already has, etc). Once he is clear on those things, he can then actually take the step of signing up. It may sound to you that this is a bit of overkill planning these things out but let's explore a little how it plays out for Sam both with the additional breakdown planning and without.

When Sam decides not to break his tasks down

Sam puts a note in his diary for Monday lunchtime to sign up for a charity event. Once he's done that, he will then download a training plan and crack on straight away!

Monday lunchtime comes around and he opens his browser and starts to search for what's available near him. There are a couple of marathons on but he's not sure about those yet as he's not sure what the training commitment would be on those. Or there's a walking event but that's in September but he's also looking to book a holiday for 2 weeks in August or September so may not be able to do that one. Oooh, now those cycling ones look really good but he doesn't have a bike yet so isn't sure how much additional cost that would introduce. Maybe this trek across Madagascar? But you need to raise a lot for that - could he do that in time? Before he knows it, his lunch break is over, so he knows he'll have to come back to this again later this evening and take another look.

Sam doesn't look at it again today. He puts off coming back to this later. It took him a lot longer than he thought it would in that first attempt on his lunchbreak so he knows he can't fit that easily into his work day as it is much too big a task for the time he has available then. He decides his only option is to look at it again after work.

When he gets home, Sam struggles to see where he can find the time to fit in the 2-3 hours of more research he now believes he needs. He was hoping that this would be a quick win, some positive action he could immediately take towards his new life but didn't expect it to be so hard to decide! And now he also thinks he's already failed as he is behind where he wanted to be already, and he's only just started! This kicks Sam into a spiral of negative thoughts - why couldn't he be more decisive, what is wrong with him?? He feels that he has no chance of sorting the bigger parts of his action plan out if he can't even do signing up for a charity event right…

Does this sound familiar?

When Sam decides to break his tasks down

Let's take a look at the same scenario with Sam but this time broken down into tasks properly. Sam has broken down the action "sign up for a charity event" into 8 tasks as follows:

1. Research types of events available,

2. Decide on preferred type of event,

3. Research training commitment needed,

4. Establish readiness timeline,

5. Identify target events,

6. Research charities affiliated to the target events,

7. Select event and charity,

8. Register.

The following Monday lunchtime, he has set himself task 1 to complete: research the types of events available, and then task 2 for Monday evening to make a decision on the event type he wants to do.

He decides to go for a half marathon and can now tick off tasks 1 and 2 as completed on schedule - immediate progress!

For Tuesday he has planned on looking at training plans. Now he knows he is going with a half marathon, he can spend a bit of time looking for books, websites or downloadable plans. He saves a couple of links and files and sees that a number of couch to half marathon plans take around 5 months and require runs 4 days a week of working up to 90 min runs at the end. Sam knows he's unlikely to get time to start this until next week as he'd need to plan it into his schedule, and he knows he's planning on being away for 2 weeks in August or September which would impact the training schedule so an event in late September or early October would be best. Tasks 3 and 4 are now ticked off his list.

On Wednesday he does a quick search for half marathons in September and October and comes up with 3 in his local area or 2 which would require travel. He decides that he would be more comfortable with a local event for his first one so shortlists the 3 local ones. Tick off task 5.

On Thursday he takes a look at some of the charities relating to the 3 events. He picks the one that feels right to him and takes a look at the sponsorship targets. One of the 3 events has an extra team vibe for his chosen charity so he selects that one. Tick off tasks 6 and 7.

On Friday he completes the sign up, plans his training in and is ready to start training. He can tick off task 8 and now feels like he's made great progress all week so his mood and energy levels are high going into the next part of his plan - training for the event.

You can see from this that by taking some time to analyse what needs to go into the activity of "sign up for a charity event" you have better control of completing the activity. You have already taken into account the types of information you might need, the interim decisions that need to be made and can therefore make sure you give yourself the right amount of mental and physical space to allow yourself to crack on and achieve it - without ending up in a tailspin that you could have prevented with a bit of work up front.

Defining Tasks

Go back to your list of high-level activities and pick one of the items that you identified as something you could action immediately. Take a good look at what tasks might be part of that action and break them down one at a time. Remember that you don't need to go overboard with the tiniest level of detail so the task is micro-planned, as this can also often be counterproductive. So back to Sam's example he was happy with "research types of event" and didn't feel the need to add subtasks like "open browser window, go to Google, etc" in there. In your project you might find that creating a greater number of tasks at a lower level of detail is what is needed as that makes sense for your particular activity, at other times you may find that a higher level works well for you. It is all about balance. You need to work out what level of detail works best for you.

Here are some further examples to help you of how activities can be broken down further:

"Book a table/pitch at a selling event" - breaks down as:

- Identify target events,

- Identify who to speak to at each target event,

- Schedule/arrange a meeting/call to confirm the booking,

- Attend the meeting/call,

- Confirm event is booked.

"Eat healthy lunches this week" - breaks down as:

- Identify specifically what healthy means,

- Are you going to buy out or make your own?

- If buy out, what are you going to buy and where from?

- If make your own, what are these going to be?

- Create a meal plan for the week, add the items to your shopping list.

- Confirm when you plan to prepare your lunch - need to get up 15 mins earlier or do that the night before?

"Go for a run 3 days a week" - breaks down as:

- Identify which days you are running,

- How long/how far is each run, which route will you take?

- Do you need to buy any equipment that you don't have already? If so, when can you get that?

- What time of day?

- Do you plan to listen to music on the run? If so, what?

- Do you need to create a playlist?

- Make sure you have a task planned to get your setup done the night before and you have enough clean clothes to make it happen for you.

"Research new career options" - breaks down as:

- Establish a list of areas you want to focus on first, what kinds of things do you want to know?

- Are you going to look online or find people to talk to in person?

- Where are you going to look?

- What outcome are you expecting from your research?

Once you have been through your list like this and broken your activities down into individual steps, you will be left with a list of short tasks that you will be able to work through quickly and easily. Ticking each one off your list will give you a sense of progress. If something crops up that is unexpected which forces you to miss a particular action then you can simply pick it up again where you left off. You don't need to abandon all progress so far and feel like the whole thing needs starting again. Another advantage to breaking things down into tasks is it helps you to identify where you have a gap in your knowledge about what you need to do. Having gaps is absolutely fine and very common when you are venturing into new areas. Knowing the specifics around any gaps will help you define what help you may need from other people or what you need to research to allow you to proceed.

Going back to Jo's example of taking more workload into her team, she had identified a whole strand of her Mind Map where she needed more information. As that entire area for her is an unknown, Jo's task list for that strand has started out as a fact-finding mission. She needs to speak to her manager to get the name and contact details of someone she can speak to about the new work coming in. She then needs to make contact with that person and set up a meeting with them and discuss what her team are going to be taking on. The output she needs from that meeting is information around the type of work, how much effort it takes each week/month, the frequency it needs to happen and what systems/process is currently used to do it. Once she has that information, Jo can build a better picture of what the next gaps are that she needs to close. She will then repeat this process until she has enough information to move forward.

For your tasks, filling in the gaps is important but do try not to fall into what I call the Information Honeypot. This is a very subtle trap that people find themselves stuck in to when they are looking to research a new thing they want to do. Some knowledge of a new area is absolutely necessary, but you always need to balance acquiring new knowledge with taking action. The people who get stuck cross the line from necessary research into almost trying to become world experts in the new area before they take any action. They have become "eternal students" and just keep learning as an excuse to not move forward. There is no point at all in learning all about in a new career choice or side project you have always wanted to do but then never actually doing anything about it. I know people who have spent years hopping from book to book, course to course, guru to guru hoping to find that one magic piece of information that will suddenly enable them to achieve what they want.

I have fallen into the Honeypot myself many, many times over the years. This was always a particular problem for me whenever I lacked self confidence in what I was doing. I would convince myself that I needed to have a qualification of some sort as a backup for me being what I aspired to be. The only way I could get myself back out was to recognise my thirst for information and qualifications for what it really was - procrastination based in fear. The cure for this was simply to take action. It is that simple. Even tiny steps within one of the activities on your task list counts as action. Keep moving forward and don't get side-tracked by feeling like you aren't able to make progress because you don't yet know all of it. You may never know all of it, no one does. Focus on what you know right now and take the best action you can with that knowledge. Trust yourself and do it.

Jo needs to make sure she keeps moving forward with her planned tasks. If she stops everything until she has ALL the information she is seeking, or pauses waiting on someone else to give this to her then she's lost control of her action plan and will fail to make any progress. The same applies to you with your plan.   Make sure you keep up momentum.

How long does a task take?

Another area people can struggle with initially is in estimating how long tasks will take to complete. Hands up here for being one of those people who would always vastly overestimate how much they can get done in any given time if I don't plan properly. This is particularly true if it is something I am just hoping to fit in around my other commitments.

> "Work expands to fill
> the time available for
> its completion."
> **Parkinson's Law**

When you have had some practice with planning tasks for yourself then you will become much better at it and can usually get it about right. What can help is to use your experience of doing something similar in the past to help you plan how long you expect a task to take. If you don't have previous experience of anything similar or if you aren't sure where to start, then what I always do as a fall-back is decide how long I want to spend doing something and work from that. So for example, for new task I will allocate 30 minutes to do it and see how far I get. It might not sound like a lot of time to start with, but you would be amazed how much you can actually get done in a focused 30 minutes with no distractions!

Time can run away really quickly if you lose focus on what you are trying to do. Research tasks and meetings with other people in particular can keep going and going if left unchecked. The easiest way to keep control of tasks like these are to be very clear on the information you need out of each session, and also to hold fast to the time limit you have set. If you give yourself 30 minutes to find out about a particular topic, then very often the whole 30 minutes is used and there is some output. If you give yourself 60 minutes to do the same thing then, as described in Parkinson's Law, the task magically expands and the whole 60 minutes is used to produce the same level of output. You can guard against this by working in shorter time bursts which will focus you better on getting exactly what it is that you need. If in doubt about how long you should allow for research, start with 30 minutes (or even 15 minutes if you are pushed for time) and then if you need more time, schedule another slot. Being focused will save you time in the long run.

7 PLANS

We are now going to build your high-level timeline and tasks into a plan that you can execute. In order to do this, we are going to look in more depth at how the tasks you have identified can slot together in the most effective sequence within your timeline. Sequencing tasks is really just a way of getting them into the right order so that you can complete each one without getting yourself stuck. Getting tasks into the right order is something that I have found that many people need a bit more help to get their head around at first but they get better at it with practice. We touched on some of this earlier with Sam's example around signing up for his first charity event, that showed why it was crucial to not only break down what you want to do into tasks, but also that getting those tasks into the right order was necessary for success. Take the time to focus on this part properly and not just rush ahead as the output is worth it.

In order to illustrate how sequencing works, I will use a really basic example from my fundraising plan: baking for a cake sale. I am sure you can easily identify the high-level sequence of activities here as 1) Prepare, 2) Bake and 3) Sell, but this starts to get more complex when you break those down further to the task level. In order to sequence tasks effectively we need to know 3 key things:

1) What needs to happen before the task,

2) What happens after the task,

3) How long each task will take.

Getting the right order

An activity that needs to happen before a particular task is known as a "predecessor" task. If this predecessor task is not completed then it will prevent the later tasks from happening. For example, a task of 'mix cake ingredients' has to come before a task of 'bake cake' - you can't bake a cake that you haven't mixed yet.

Tasks that follow on from another task and that depend on its completion are called "successors". An example of a successor to the 'bake cake' task would be cutting it into portions - you need to have a completed cake before you can portion it.

Once you have a good grasp on what each task's predecessors and successors are, you can also identify which tasks are critical to complete within your plan and those that are more of a 'nice to have'. You can also readily identify which tasks could be brought forward in your sequence to start earlier. A great example of this would be to tell people that you are doing a cake sale ahead of time as it gives people a chance to plan to come along and buy cake!

Below I have shared an extract of the plan I used for my cake sales. I had already done some work around identifying an event and worked out other details about how much I expected to sell. This part of the plan below covers the remaining tasks to undertake the cake sale itself. The first graphic shows my initial task list (labelled A-U) and the second graphic shows how I then sequenced those tasks into an effective plan.

PREP:
A. Confirm what to sell.
B. Estimate number of portions to be made.
C. Find recipes.
D. Work out ingredient cost.
E. Buy ingredients.

BAKE:
F. Identify portion size.
G. Identify number of batches needed.
H. Identify how much time needed per batch.
I. Mix cakes.
J. Bake cakes.
K. Cooling and decorating time.
L. Cut into portions.
M. Package cakes.

SELL:
N. Identify type and quantity of packaging.
O. Buy packaging required.
P. Determine selling price.
Q. Identify transportation method.
R. Advertise cake sale in advance.
S. Plan advertising at the event itself.
T. Create/obtain posters/pull up banner.
U. Create price list.

At the moment you can see that there are 3 separate lists - one each for Prep, Bake and Sell. If this was a regular To Do List you might be tempted to work through the lists in the order shown i.e. work through the lists of Prep, Bake and Sell in that order. However, if we did that we would quickly run into problems.

One obvious example would be that the cakes are baked and cut into portions but we haven't yet started to look at packaging as that is on the Sell list. There is a chance here that you won't be able to find suitable packaging immediately and so will have cakes going stale before your event. A better way of sequencing the tasks would be to look at how we can combine tasks from each of the three lists and create a new running order that works better. I have done this below and have left the labels in place so you can see how the order of the tasks has changed:

As you can see, these are the same tasks as before, they are just in a different order that allows them to be worked through more efficiently. Tasks associated with a later activity (Sell) but that make sense to do earlier are brought forward. This then allows all three task lists to be worked on in parallel and means that and predecessor and successor tasks are done at the right time even if they originally belonged to one of the other lists.

Adding some timings

The next thing we need to do to build out your plan is add in how long we are expecting each task to take. You will already have some estimations from earlier so now just need to check and confirm your estimates against any new information you have received. For example, I know that making a batch of flapjacks takes me around 40 minutes to weigh out the ingredients, mix them and bake them. You may have decided upon scheduling yourself 30 minutes to go on a run, or 2 hours to take a trip to the gym, or an hour to review and update your CV for that job application. An initial estimate of time is absolutely fine at this stage, you can easily test and refine as you go.

When I first started writing I had no idea how long it would take me to write a book. What I did was measure how long on average it took me to write 1000 words. I then looked at what a sensible word target would be for a book in the genre that I was writing and worked out how many sessions it would take to write that number of words. That gave me a starting point for how many writing tasks I would need to plan in to complete the first draft of my book. I would then measure progress as I went along so I could keep an eye on whether I would need more or less time than I had originally planned. That same approach of trying something, measuring and using that to plan with works for many different types of tasks. This works particularly well when you have a task that needs to be repeated several times to achieve your goal - like training sessions if you are working towards a fitness goal, or number of cake sales needed to hit a fundraising target. Once you know what length of time one set of those tasks is expected to take, you can apply that to all of them.

Work through your own task list now and play with it to see how it would be sequenced best. If this is new to you, you might find it easier to put each task onto a piece of paper or post it note and then play with re-ordering them. When you are happy with that order then you can write down your tasks into your tracker of choice (I have some suggestions for these coming up later). Exactly the same principles apply to planning and sequencing whether your project requires a fairly small number of tasks or whether it is more complex. If you are tackling a large or lengthy project, simply break that down into chunks and follow the same advice as in the sections above - identify what needs doing at a task level, work out how long you need for it, put it into your plan in the most effective sequence.

Before we finish with this section (and before you crack on with executing your plan), there are two more things we need to pay attention to. First is identifying the priority tasks in the plan. These are the ones that have a number of successors so that not completing these particular tasks means that you will miss your goal. It is worth highlighting these so that when we come to scheduling tasks into your day you are aware of the impact of not completing them as planned. The other thing to look at is what resources or help do you need to be able to get your task done? Examples of resources could be access to a phone to call someone, a PC/laptop/iPad to write on, a kitchen to bake in, a gym kit to go running in. Examples of help that you might need could be getting an extra pair of hands to help with your cake sale, or a personal trainer to push you towards your fitness goals. Note each of these down against each task as that will help in terms of how we schedule these into your day in the next section.

8 RISKS

If you have followed along and completed the steps in the last section, you have by now created a high-level plan - well done! Getting this specific about what you need to do is quite an achievement and has greatly increased your chance of success. You probably think that you can now sail merrily along, ticking off tasks as you go until you reach the goal you have now set for yourself. I hate to break it to you, but if it was as simple as that, everyone would achieve everything they set out to do. Your plan may work right now on paper but in order for you to really use it as a tool to complete your project, you need to know how to flex the plan when it is inevitably challenged by your everyday life.

> *"The best laid plans of mice and men often go awry."*
> **Robert Burns**
> (Adapted from 'To a Mouse')

Research shows that a little thought and preparation in advance around how you would handle an issue that crops up means that you will be much more effective at dealing with it should it arise.

As an example, interviews with survivors of plane crashes have shown that the common element is that the people who got out quickly had planned what they would do in an emergency situation - which exit they would aim for, what route they would take to get there and what the alternative plan was if that exit was blocked. Thinking through up front what they would do if something went wrong was key to their survival. Your project is unlikely to lead you to face such extreme risks but the principle holds firm - give some thought about how you will handle challenges to achieving your project before something goes wrong. This section is going to give you the tools you need to identify and prepare for challenges in advance.

There are two main sources for challenges that could derail your project: external sources and internal sources. External sources are things you have no influence over like family emergencies and cancelled meetings or events. If your project involves working a lot with other people, it is likely that most of your challenges will be part of the external category. Internal sources are by far the most common for personal development projects (even though you might try to convince yourself that these are external and therefore out of your control as we shall explore later). In both cases, spending some time up front to think about the types of challenge that you might meet, what impact those challenges might have to your plan and how you can overcome them will massively increase your chances of going on to complete your plan and achieve success in your project.

The Outside Adversary

Let's start by looking at external challenges and how you can prepare for those. Take a look through the tasks you have got in your plan, the plan itself and your overall project goal and note down the things that could happen to negatively impact each of them. To illustrate with my fundraising example - I might sell very little at the table top sales, one or more events I've planned might be cancelled, I might get no interest in corporate sponsorship, I might be short of the fundraising target at the end of the 9 months. You get the idea. Rather than deal with each of these if or when they happen, I spent some time planning out what my strategy would be for handling each situation if it came up.

Let me show you what I mean with the example of selling less at a table-top sale than planned: If I was budgeting to make £100 at the first sale but only took £50 then I would be left with 2 problems to fix - excess stock left over and being short on my target. So what could I do about this? In terms of the excess stock - would it be possible to sell the excess stock elsewhere? If so, where could I get lined up as a possible fall-back option? For the shortfall on the expected takings, could I fit additional table tops in? Run 8 instead of the 4 I had planned to? If so, where else could I run those? The answers to these questions let me create a mini plan that I could use in terms of contingency if needed. It also allowed me to put a couple of other tasks into my main plan to look for additional table top opportunities that I could book onto just in case.

Picking back up with Jo and her project to absorb more workload into her team, Jo spent some time analysing the challenges that she could face with regards the new work her team were to be responsible for following a merger. If you remember from her mind mapping exercise, Jo had a number of different areas that she needed to find out more about before she could create a plan to bring in the extra work. Jo decided that each of these unknowns was a potential risk to her project, so she jotted down what could negatively result from each one and how she would deal with each if it arose. For example, if the new work required data held in IT systems that her team don't yet have access to, could she identify a person outside of her team to work with to download and share the data they need? Similarly for Sam, an external challenge for him in his half-marathon training could be an injury picked up on a training run that requires several days of rest. How would he manage that in his training plan? Does he have room to repeat a week in the plan whilst he recovers? Are there other forms of exercise he could do to maintain fitness without compromising his recovery - swimming for example? For both Jo and Sam, planning these things out at a high level meant that they had contingency plans to fall back on if the need arose rather than being blindsided by something unexpected happening and then trying to recover their plan in a panic.

The Enemy Within

Now on to the types of challenges which are most likely to be responsible for derailing your plan - those that are internally generated. This means they are things that you (or your brain) throw in your way to sabotage your progress. You don't believe that you would do that to yourself? Let's see if any of this sounds familiar to you? You are super-enthusiastic about your plan and what you are going to achieve and are raring to go! You are working through your task list and making good progress with what you have set yourself to do. A few days in, you notice that your enthusiasm has waned slightly as you realise you are going to have to work hard to get what you want. You notice that it starts to get just a teeny bit tougher to work on that task today or go for that run. The voice in your head (you know the one) will start to make itself heard. It will start off with by saying sensible-sounding things like: "You did such a great job at this last week that you really deserve today off". "You have a free afternoon coming up later in the week so you can catch up then". "Go ahead and watch that show you love as a treat tonight instead of heading to the gym - one session missed won't hurt". "If you really don't feel like working on your project today then don't worry about it - you can catch up with it tomorrow and do extra when you are feeling fresher and your ideas are flowing better".

Don't fall for any of it.

This is your current self just trying to be sneaky. It is you trying to use what sounds like logic to persuade yourself to deviate from your plan. It is your fear of change acting like the wolf in sheep's clothing to knock you off track. Deviations from your plan will absolutely happen due to external risks and circumstances outside of your control, but these are usually one-off events and you can usually replan around them to get yourself back on track.

This inner voice however is a different beast altogether. If you give in to it even a tiny bit then you will exploit your own weaknesses to stop your progress and ultimately fail to achieve the things you say you want. I bet you are a bit like me, you have achieved a number of things so far in your life that you are proud of, but there are also a good number of things that you set out to do to but fell short due to lack of action. I don't play a musical instrument for example, nor am I fluent in Spanish/Japanese/Welsh or any other language I've tried to learn since leaving school. I am not able to run 10k without stopping (very) frequently. My first small side-line business also essentially failed as I dabbled rather that doing the things I should have done. I am sure if I think hard I can come up with more examples like this in my personal closet of failures. I am sure you have a similar closet of your own too.

Unless you take consistent action towards achieving your goals you will never hit any of them. I own my failed goals as I am absolutely responsible for causing myself to fail in each case as I stopped taking action. Failure happened either because I picked something that I didn't really want to do (my failed side-line business), or because I allowed that inner voice to muscle in and influence both my planning and my execution of that plan. In my experience, you need to ignore/shut down/drown out that inner voice from the very start. If you say "yes" to any one of its sensible-sounding little deviations from your plan, then you have opened the door to failure.

Closing the door can be much more difficult than just learning to ignore that voice. If we take my most recent attempt at "becoming a runner" a couple of years ago, I did everything right at the start - I created a training plan, found a race I was going to enter (actually paid to enter it!) bought new running gear to prove to myself I was serious, found a realistic training plan, slotted it into my routine and started training. 6 weeks into the training plan I let the door open, just a crack, and skipped a session.

Skipping that one session meant I then had to replan the next week's sessions to get back on track. I thought to myself, as I was replanning anyway, I could really do with moving this other one due to a family birthday, but that's fine I'll just work sessions in for the next couple of weeks. Having replanned once clearly meant I wouldn't have a problem doing it again, right?

A month later I was on week 8 of the training plan rather than week 10, but that's fine, plenty of time to catch up! Another month later I was on week 10 of the plan rather than week 14…

This is where the voice tries a new tactic. "Well you know you are a month off schedule now, that's going to be tough on you, how about you find a later race to enter? No point trying to cram in any additional training as you'll just end up compromising rest days and give yourself an injury". I told you there was sneaky logic in there! It can also start to press your most vulnerable buttons (this voice is part of you remember so like a spiteful sibling it knows exactly what to press for maximum impact) - "you may as well forget about doing this or maybe find a 5k you can train for, don't overstretch yourself as remember you aren't a real runner, you aren't fit like all the other people who will be in the race. You know people who do real running who can do a 10k in sub-50 minutes, you will look really slow crawling in at 80 minutes and they'll all be laughing at you…" Hopefully you get my point?

I had the same battle writing my first book (this one!). Although part of me has always wanted to write, the rest of me has never really believed that it was possible for "someone like to me" to do. When I decided that this was really what I wanted to do and I created my writing project (using the exact same processes as we went through earlier in this book), each time I sat down to write my inner voice would chime in at me with things like "you are setting a target of 2500 words per day? So high? Wouldn't something more modest be better for a first attempt at a novel?" or "You'll be much too tired writing for 2-3 hours a night after work, wouldn't it be better to maybe just put a couple of writing sessions a week in instead so you don't tire yourself out, after all you are working to your own deadlines here so you can take as long as you like?" or "You've already written loads so wouldn't it be better to go back and make those perfect before continuing?", and so on.

Each and every time I sat down to write my inner voice would start talking me out of it.

Each and every time I had to take a moment to consider what my inner voice was saying, weigh that up against my goal and see whether or not it was something I wanted to entertain or not.

Each and every time I had to fight myself to make sure I cracked on and actually did what I had planned to do. How nuts is that?

> *"If you hear a voice within you say 'You cannot paint', then by all means paint and that voice will be silenced."*
> **Vincent van Gogh**

Over time I realised that I could take less time out of my writing to ponder the temptations my inner voice was throwing in my path, by asking myself a simple question:

Is this something that is going to take me one step closer to or one step further away from my goal?

I found that remembering to do this enables me to stop my inner voice in its tracks most of the time and then I can get on with what I had planned for that day. Another technique that also works for me when my inner voice tries to get me to squirm out of doing the task I am supposed to be doing is to take a journal and write out what my reason was to be excused from doing the task as planned. I got the idea for this whilst reminiscing with a friend about school days where you had to have a reason for missing things like PE classes or for forgetting your homework. Genuine reasons were typically given to teachers with no trace of embarrassment, but made up excuses were a lot harder to give without feeling uncomfortable as you knew you weren't really telling the truth. I discovered that I get that same uncomfortable feeling if I write a 'not-100%-genuine' reason for skipping out on what I have planned to do into my journal. I can therefore catch myself in the act just by looking out for that feeling. This has made my success rate at actually doing what I say I am going to do much higher. See if doing something similar helps you manage your inner voice.

Once you have identified a few things that might be risks to you following your plan and achieving your goal, make note and keep those notes handy to refer to should you need to replan.

End of Section Checklist

> You have created a list of what could go wrong.
>
> You have identified the specific actions you could take in the event of a problem occurring.
>
> You know who you can call on for help or support if needed.

Part Three

CREATE
SPACE

9 PLAN & GO

You've done all the hard work in the previous chapters and are now ready to take all of your notes and bring them all together into "The Plan" that you can go and run with. If you are creating a project plan as part of your job, then the standard approach in your company is likely to be to create and manage it using Microsoft Project. This enables you to build up your task list and easily link tasks together with their predecessors and successors. The software can do a whole lot more than that, and in my years of experience as a project manager, I have never needed to use more than half of its functions to get the job done! If you aren't creating a work-based plan or your company allows you freedom to manage things in your own way, then there are a number of tools you can use for this so there will be something to suit how you like to work.

There are a number of options you can explore depending on the tools you have available to you, whether you prefer pen and paper or an electronic solution, whether you are likely to be in one location or on the go a lot, and what level of detail you need at your fingertips during your day.

The temptation here can be to go out and buy the latest and greatest planner or a fancy piece of software but you can manage yourself and your plan perfectly well with some simple tools. For my personal projects, I like to use a combination of paper-based and electronic planning tools and trackers as that fits in with my lifestyle. Here are some of my favourites:

Paper-based Planners

A quick browse through a stationery shop or on Amazon will show you that there are thousands of different types of planners and diaries on the market. I have always used some sort of paper planner to keep track of things I need to do - this started off with pocket diaries in my teens, migrated to a Filofax when I started working and now I buy an A5 size notebook that I like and use that as a custom bullet journal.

A pocket diary is great for being able to plan tasks and appointments in for specific days and is also easy to take out and about to refer to on the go. If you are brand new to having a level of planning in your life then I would absolutely recommend getting one of these and using that to schedule your tasks to start with. Please use a pen rather than a pencil to add your tasks into the diary as, psychologically, this makes them a "firm" commitment for you rather than something that is just "pencilled in". I would also suggest switching to a pocket diary and pen if you are used to adding tasks and appointments to your smartphone calendar but find yourself struggling to get those things done. With smartphone calendars it is really easy to get distracted by other notifications you see when you look at your phone which then prevents you actioning your task as planned - something that cannot happen with a pocket diary!

Actually writing your task into your diary in ink also helps you with accountability as you can see at a glance how many times you've had to shuffle or reschedule a task that you need to do. If you notice you've had to move tasks a number of times then it can be a signal to look at either your scheduling, the size of the tasks you are creating or your motivation to complete the task and nip that in the bud before it becomes a larger problem.

One thing I did find limiting with the pocket diary was that I needed to keep an overall plan somewhere else as there wasn't an option to do this within the diary itself. To start with I used to keep a folded piece of paper with my project details on within the pocket diary, and I also used a calendar or wall planner to draw out my timeline on, so I could keep the overall view of what I was doing in mind.

I switched up from a diary and wall planner to a Filofax as it became more important to me to have a fully portable tracking and planning tool as I was travelling around quite a lot at the time. As well as the standard diary-style inserts, I bought other inserts for my Filofax for monthly and yearly planners and also some blank pages so I could take notes and keep them all together within the same binder.

These days I use a hardback A5 notebook as a hybrid planner and bullet journal and I set that up exactly as I need to match the projects I have on at the time. It starts life as a plain A5 notebook and I draw in whatever combination of calendar, weekly planner and notes pages that I need when I need them. I can stick with high-level "do task x on this day" entries, or if I need more focus, I can also draw in some pages where I plan my day out in more detail and I can assign tasks or activities to specific timeslots. I use other pages within the notebook in the more traditional bullet journal sense by capturing bullet point notes or additional tasks each day that I can then add to my plan and schedule in as appropriate. I really love the flexibility of this system so if this sounds like it might interest you then go and check out *bulletjournal.com* for more information.

If you Google bullet journals in general, just a word of caution. There are a number of highly creative people who take great pride in decorating their bullet journal pages with colour, drawings, calligraphy and stickers which can look beautiful but can also be a bit intimidating to look at, particularly if you are new to planning. There is no need to spend time making your planner or notebook into a work of art as, first and foremost, it is a planning tool to help support you getting what you need to do done on time.

There are also a number of excellent done-for-you planners on the market that have spaces to record monthly and weekly goals as well as daily tasks and also offer you space to review progress or capture your thoughts. These vary in size, price and layout and it can take some time to research them all and see if any strike you as a good fit for what you would like to use it for. If you are new to planning and worry about getting something overcomplicated that you might struggle to use, then I would stick with a basic pocket diary to start with as that works perfectly well for most people most of the time.

Electronic Planners

As with the paper planners, there are a vast number of planning tools, apps and software out there that all promise to make your life easier, make you more productive and help you achieve all your goals. In practice, most of these are variations on creating a list of tasks you need to do, adding dates to those tasks and scheduling a reminder to do the task. Some are easier to use than others and I am a great believer in keeping it simple - if you are spending more time managing the tools you are using to plan your tasks than you are actually doing the tasks then there is something wrong somewhere!

Starting quite simply, the most basic electronic planner is a spreadsheet program. This can be Excel, which comes as part of Microsoft Office, Apple's Numbers program or one of the freeware versions like Calc by LibreOffice. These programs are really designed to do so many more things than most of us will ever use them for, but they are also a great way to create lists. I like to use a spreadsheet to record my overall plan and usually have three tabs in my project file:

1. The first tab gives me the overall timeline which I make quite simply by setting up like a calendar and colouring in cells within the date ranges of my various activities to produce a visual overview of my plan.

2. The second tab I use for my actual task list and I add additional columns for the date the task is scheduled, when it was completed, any notes I need to record against it and also whether I can now mark it as complete. I use the sorting and filtering functions in the software to help manage

this tab so I can see what tasks I have coming up to do in the next few days. I transfer these tasks into my bullet journal so I can keep them with me at all times but you could easily print this list off and use that as your weekly schedule.

3. The third tab is where I keep notes of my targets and why so that they are handy for reference. I also put my risk and contingency notes into this tab.

I find using a spreadsheet in combination with my bullet journal works for me, but you could use just the spreadsheet as a planner as you could store it in a product like Dropbox so that it is accessible from all your devices anywhere you have an internet or mobile data connection if that is how you prefer to work.

If you are comfortable using a more online solution as a planner then you can also use various calendar apps to both capture your overall timeline and also schedule your specific tasks each day. Google Calendar and iCal both have similar features - you can set up time blocks for specific tasks, set reminders and also use integrated task lists to manage your plans. If you want to explore other tools that offer planning solutions then a quick search will show you that there is a lot of choice available - some free, some paid. Most come with instructional videos and free trial versions or permanently free 'lite' versions that allow you to get used to the tool and see if it is a good fit before you decide to purchase the full version. Trello and Asana are popular ones to take a look at although Asana is really more geared towards having a team working towards the same project. Evernote is also a good one to look at. I use that mostly to collect research and for when I am doing a braindump around a new project but it does give you the option to create checklists and you can access it across two devices on the free version so you can work on your PC/iPad and have the same notes and checklist available to you on your smartphone when you are out and about.

If this is a work-based project or you have your own Office 365 subscription, then you will have access to Microsoft Office products like Outlook and OneNote as well as Excel. Outlook is predominantly thought of as an email client but it has a built-in calendar you can use for time-blocking and creating your visual timeline as well as a task list you can set reminders for so you can also use it as a basic planning tool. OneNote has similar functionality to Evernote and is great for organising project notes. One great feature of OneNote is that you can tag any piece of text with a "To-Do" flag within your OneNote notebook and it can pull them all together into a single "To-Do List" page which also integrates with Outlook. I have used this feature countless times over the years for projects at work.

Ultimately whatever method you use to record your plan is down to your own personal preference. If you are more comfortable using paper or would much prefer to have it on your smartphone or computer, then choose something accordingly. The most important thing is to get it set up properly from the start with two main things: a timeline view so you can see what needs to happen when and keep the big picture in mind; and a task view so you can see what tasks are scheduled in for when so that you see them and remember to do them.

10 FIT IT IN

The next part of this book will help you take the plan you have created and fit it into your life so that you can actually achieve it. Do you ever find you have great focus and strong motivation, but you really struggle to find the time to actually do the tasks you've set yourself? As the tasks slip, your progress slips and you start to lose confidence in your ability to actually do this. You'd really like to get your project completed but you also have a huge amount of other daily and weekly commitments that also need to be done, so how do you find that time that you need?

This really stumped me when I started to look at doing my own projects. I work full time, as does my husband, we have two kids and a house to manage so a lot of the available hours in a day are already accounted for. I did what a lot of people do to start with - go and find some books or websites to read to try and pick up tips that I could use to fit more into my day. What I found was that a lot of the traditional productivity books relied on me implementing a whole new philosophy in my life to unlocks some superstar level organisational skills. Those new philosophies came with prescriptive processes that needed to be followed religiously or the whole thing fell apart and you end up in a mess. They are also usually aimed at improving office-based productivity, focusing on things like managing your email, prioritising what work you need to do first and storing all pieces of information that you might need at some point into a master task list or "second brain" so you don't forget or lose anything. I have always liked the idea of having that zen-like calm control over my life and activities, but then I am reminded that my life isn't just office-based and invariably chaos sometimes happens - particularly when you have a young family.

An alternative to the productivity models that I found worth exploring is the 'life hack'. If you aren't familiar with these, 'hacks' are basically tips and tricks that you can use to help you do something more quickly. There are loads of websites dedicated to various types of hack - food, fitness, home, personal development, etc. and you can generally find these easily with a quick online search. Personally, I find some of the hacks to be really great, some not so great and some pretty gimmicky for very little return so you will have to do a bit of sifting through to find something that looks like it's worth trying. I have been reading about and trying new ways to stretch my days for nearly 20 years so in the following section will share what has worked for me and how I fit my projects into an already busy life so hopefully it gives you some ideas you can use.

Making Time

If you have few other demands on your time, then you can simply lift the tasks off your plan and schedule them in to the relevant day then go ahead and do them. However, if you are like most people who have to juggle work, family, home and also like to sleep now and again, fitting in what you need to get done for your project is rarely easy but it can be done. We all have 24 hours in any given day but it is possible to make additional productive time if you think creatively about it. Through trial and error, these are the things that have worked for me:

1) Changing your waking hours.

The idea behind this is that you either get up earlier or stay up later so that you get some uninterrupted time working on your own project without having other priorities encroaching on your time. The most popular version of this is getting up an hour or two earlier than usual and progressing your own project before the rest of the household wakes up. This can work brilliantly for exercise programmes and creative projects as you can crack on with your workout or your craft before your brain is awake enough to talk you out of it!

Early starts are also really good for kicking off a new personal development mindset as you learn to prioritise and focus on the new you first thing every day. If this is something you want to take a deeper look at I can recommend the Miracle Morning by Hal Elrod as a great starting point. I do a 30-day stint of Miracle Morning a couple of times a year when I need a boost. If you have kids, the early mornings can also be a great option as you are able to prioritise your needs when they aren't up and about.

If you know that you really aren't a morning person at all, or your kids are young and seem to possess psychic powers that mean they get up seconds after you do no matter how early, the other option is to find time in the evening instead. Think about what you currently do in the evenings and see where you can make some changes to enable you to have some time to work on your project, or just stay up an hour later if that suits you best.

When my kids were young, early mornings were never child-free so I had to adapt to using time in the evenings instead to get my projects done. I used to put them to bed and then stay upstairs working in my bedroom for an hour or so whilst they went to sleep. They both went through a phase of thinking they were missing out on some mysterious and exciting grown-up stuff when they were put to bed and my husband and I went back downstairs (in reality we were basically just sitting down with a cup of tea after our long day!). This led to it taking them ages to settle down at night. When I stayed upstairs in my room, that had the added advantage of them realising that there was nothing else exciting going on in the house so they would fall asleep quicker too.

One important thing to remember if you are looking at adjusting your waking hours at either end of the day, you need to ensure you are still getting enough sleep. It is possible to burn the candle at both ends for a short period of time but doing that longer term just leads to exhaustion and burnout.

2) Hidden Time.

At one point several years ago I realised that even with adjusting my waking hours I was still not managing to get what I wanted to do done each day, so I sat down and mapped out where I spent my time each day over the course of a week. What I discovered really surprised me!

My routine was as follows: a typical week day for me would be get up, get showered & unearth something to wear, grab some toast or cereal and then jump in the car to drive to work. Lunch would be walk out to a local sandwich shop for food. Finishing work for the day would mean sitting for an age in commuter traffic. Getting home in the evening after a long day would start with my husband and I rummaging in the fridge to see what we could make for dinner. Finally sitting down to eat around 8pm, collapsing on the sofa for a couple of hours then heading to bed just to start over again tomorrow. Weekends would be unplanned apart from laundry and the weekly trip to the supermarket.

There never seemed to be time to do anything other than work, nothing was getting done at home (we had bought a house that could politely be described as a "fixer-upper") and both of us were getting stressed out not able to progress our projects (such as sorting the house out), finding time for hobbies, going out etc.

On analysing my routine, I could see that a lot of time was being wasted, particularly when it came to how I managed my meals. I realised that by not taking the time to plan out my food purchasing and preparation properly was resulting in my lunch breaks being spent going out to buy food (2.5 hours a week), at least 2 hours a night were needed to work out what to eat and then cook it (14 hours a week), plus a weekly meander around the supermarket with no clear idea of what to buy took a couple of hours every Saturday. This meant that I was spending around 18 hours a week just feeding myself - which is equivalent to having a part time job!

I started to do a weekly meal plan every Saturday morning which generated a very prescriptive shopping list (a weekly habit that I've now been doing for more than 15 years) which cut my time spent at the supermarket by two-thirds, evening meal prep time halved and I started taking a lunch to work which meant I could work on my own projects during my lunch break instead of spending it going out to buy something to eat.

Your routine may be completely different to mine, or you might identify with parts of it. Either way I urge you to review your days and weeks and look for the hidden minutes. How many small changes can you make to free up additional time? Maybe you could find some way of doing one of the tasks on your project on your commute, or when you are waiting for an appointment? Maybe you could stop watching TV shows as they are broadcast every day and put aside 3-4 evenings a week to progress your project. You can then watch your shows later on catch-up on a designated TV evening instead?

3) Grouping Tasks.

Time blocking is a well-established office productivity method. Basically, it means you have certain activities scheduled for certain days of the week or at certain times in your working day so that you get your work done efficiently and on time. I had been doing variations on this in my day job for years when I decided to apply the same to my home life to see if that helped me use my time more effectively. I started quite simply at first and themed my days around what tasks I needed to get done in that week i.e. Mondays might be Phonecall days, Tuesdays might be Research days, etc. As I got used to working with my time in that way I refined this approach and had a number of themes running during each day which I would track in my planner. I personally still keep my time-blocking quite simple. What themes I use or when they are scheduled varies depending on what projects I currently have on the go but at the moment these are as follows:

Week days:

> Commute = learning time. I typically listening to podcasts, audiobooks or other training I have downloaded to my iPod whilst enjoying the inevitable traffic jams I am stuck in each morning and evening.
>
> Daytime = short tasks. Reviewing my daily plan. Sending quick emails, messages and

doing short pieces of research on my phone on my lunch break. Or jotting down ideas for things I want to action later.

Evening = longer tasks. Anything that will take a couple of hours or so to do. I have nights for my weekly review, volunteering, writing, project work and family time. What is actually planned on any given evening varies from week to week but is always planned into one theme per evening.

Weekends:

Daytime = home and family time in the main with a couple of hours of project time set aside each day.

Evenings = time blocked for down time only as it is really important to take time off to recharge.

Earlier in the book I recommended that you make a note of the resources you will need to help you complete each of your tasks. If you remember this could be a phone, access to the internet (via a PC/laptop/smartphone), a particular place or a particular person. Having this information available for each task helps you to group them together and so you can readily identify the tasks that you can do in a particular themed time block. For example, when I was ringing round to find venues for a charity gig I was organising, I would plan a phonecall slot and do a number of them back to back. If I couldn't get through to one of the venues and had to leave a voicemail, I also had the details of other phone tasks with me (such as calling a printer to discuss the promotional posters and tickets) so I could make the most of the rest of the time I had blocked out.

The best thing that time blocking has given me is visibility around what my week looks like, so I can plan better and make sure I am prepared in advance for each themed block of time. Knowing how much time I have per time block also helps me to focus on getting my tasks done rather than spending the time faffing about.

Going back to Parkinson's Law, have you ever noticed that if you are given a deadline of getting something done by the end of the week that it can take you a whole week to get around to doing something with it? If you are struggling to think of a recent example here, think back to your school days and how you managed your homework. Most people given a week to write an essay would end up dabbling with it for most of the week and then writing it in a couple of hours the night before it was due to be handed in. However, do you remember when you had to write a similar essay as part of an exam, you were able to produce it within the time allowed in the exam as you were forced to focus?

Look for the little pieces of spare time and use those as focused blocks of time with a hard deadline. Using these short blocks consistently really adds up over time. When I wrote my first book I was also working full time, running a household and also volunteering for charity. On the face of it, I had next to no time available to do something as apparently time consuming as write a book. But I managed it.

The secret behind that was doing exactly what I have just outlined - finding short blocks of time and making best use of them. During the week, these blocks were usually in an evening slot once the kids were in bed. Some nights I only had 30 minutes available, other nights I managed a couple of hours. At weekends, I had to fit in all the household things like food shopping, laundry, cleaning, spending time with the kids, some downtime, etc but also made time to sit down to write for as much time as I could manage each day. This is a lot less time than a full-time author would have to work on their books, but being consistent and showing up at every possible opportunity to write meant I successfully completed my book and met my goal.

You can use that exact same approach for anything you also have on your goal list. This is one of the reasons why I ask you to break your plan down into small tasks - so that you can then fit those things more easily into small windows of time and make consistent progress rather than trying to find a 2-3 hour time block you don't have. By all means if you find a bigger window then get some more of your tasks done in that window but plan it as a series of small tasks with short breaks in between, as you will find that you are more productive by doing that.

The key themes in what I have outlined above are consistency and routine. Although most people like to treat their non-working time as completely unstructured so it doesn't feel like work, creating your own routines and sticking to them is essential for achieving success with your personal projects. I am not talking about hard-structuring your days with military precision but having some gentle, regular routine to what you do really helps you to get things done effectively as we shall be looking into more in the next section.

11 ROUTINE THAT WORKS

Creating a routine for yourself is one of the most important things you can do to help you achieve your projects. Having regular things that you do daily and weekly helps to create positive habits that will ultimately help you complete your project successfully. Giving some thought to creating and implementing a routine that works for you is definitely worth the effort. If you are anything like me and have spent years trying to shoe-horn a whole lot of additional tasks into your life or give yourself an inflexible structure to work within, you will find that sooner or later it all goes wrong and you are back to missing tasks and not moving your projects forward. My advice is to start with some small changes at first and then build up from there until you have something that works for your lifestyle. To give you some ideas, I have taken you through some of my routines and also some examples from Jo's life.

We have already discussed the weekly review of your plan to check progress, upcoming tasks and to address any slips. As a minimum, you need to add this to the routine you create. Pick a day of the week that works best for you and then schedule that time into your planner. I typically do my review on Monday nights but if I have something else planned on a particular Monday then I just bring it forward to Sunday or shift it back to Tuesday but I rarely skip it all together as it is now a habitual part of my week.

In addition to reviewing my current projects, I also like to use my weekly review time to spend some time thinking about what completing each of my projects means to me and taking time to reconnect with what I am doing. I find that this helps me stop getting distracted by other things and losing focus. If you feel that you need to reconnect more frequently with your projects then by all means create yourself a daily routine for this. Creating an affirmation or simple statement that you can read every day can be really helpful here. It doesn't have to be anything particularly profound - just something that reminds you what you are aiming for.

When I was getting prepared for my Everest trek I would have classed myself as "passably fit" but knew there was a lot of work I needed to do in order to get myself in better shape for 3 weeks of hiking in the Himalayas. Alongside my fundraising project that I mentioned earlier, I also had a "Get Rachel Fit" project to essentially get me from "Couch to Base Camp" in a period of 10 months. I set up a workout plan that ran from January to October (the trek started on October 13th) and comprised workouts 3 days per week through to September when they then moved to daily workouts to coincide with a social media campaign to push the last part of my fundraising. The only time of day I could realistically fit these sessions in was by getting up at 5am 3 days a week which was really hard to do, especially for someone not used to regular exercise!

My inner voice and I had several battles a week about why skipping training was a great idea so I ensured I had a daily routine of checking in with my plan (my exercise schedule), my desired outcome (being fit enough to do all the walking I needed to do) and why I was doing this (for the people who had contributed to my fund, and also not wanting to look silly and lag behind everyone else!). To make it fun, I put a picture of Dory, from the film Finding Nemo, on my phone with her catchphrase "Just keep swimming" and that acted as a daily reminder for me to keep going.

My routine at that time ran as follows:

Mondays:

      Get up at 6am and take a few minutes to

check in with Dory.

Get ready for work/get kids up/make packed lunch from meal plan

Listen to an inspirational audiobook or podcast on my morning commute

30 min slot over lunch to progress the task scheduled for that day

Audiobook or podcast in the car on the way home

Cook from meal plan

Family time

Weekly review and refine plan for the coming week

Tuesdays and Thursdays:

Get up at 5am and do planned workout

Take a few minutes to check in with Dory

Get ready for work/get kids up/make packed lunch from meal plan

Audiobook or podcast in the car to work

30 min slot over lunch to progress the task scheduled for that day

Audiobook or podcast in the car to home

Cook from meal plan

Family time

Complete task scheduled for that evening

Wednesdays and Fridays:

Get up at 6am and take a few minutes to check in with Dory.

Get ready for work/get kids up/make packed lunch from meal plan

Audiobook or podcast in the car to work

30 min slot over lunch to progress the task scheduled for that day

Audiobook or podcast in the car to home

Cook from meal plan

Family time

Complete task scheduled for that evening (Friday evenings always scheduled as downtime)

Saturdays:

Get up at 5am and do planned workout

Take a few minutes to check in with Dory

Weekly meal planning session

Supermarket visit

Family time

Complete task scheduled for that day

Sundays:

Downtime & Family time

Complete any tasks scheduled for that day.

That routine provided enough structure to ensure I could focus on my projects but wasn't so restrictive that it was hard to sustain. I could flex it around family commitments but still maintain that level of consistency that is so important to achieving a goal. You will notice that I have made sure to block out some down time within my weekly routine. When you are trying to do something new around your existing commitments it can be really difficult to not throw yourself in to what you are doing and let it consume every spare minute of your time. I must stress how important regular breaks are to prevent burnout. If you have a longer length task to do in any given day make sure you also make the time to step away from your task for a few minutes every hour.

Have a break...

It can be really tempting to just push through and keep working on your project - I have been guilty of this in the past and do sometimes lapse and do this in the present also! Our culture today is geared towards producing faster, working harder and a "sleep when you're dead" attitude but whilst this is possible to do in short bursts, it is not a sustainable long-term strategy for anyone as at some point you will crash and burn.

When I was working with Jo around developing her plan and routine I was conscious that the culture at her workplace was scarily similar to mine in that it didn't really allow for breaks. It was ruled by the Microsoft Outlook calendar - if you weren't blocked out in a meeting then you were "available". Too much time showing as available and people would inevitably try and fill it for you. It was pretty common for me to be in back to back meetings for a full working day, including working through what should have been my lunch break. As my work environment evolved to embrace virtual working then it wasn't physical meetings to attend with at least a short walk to a new meeting room before the next one, but a Skype call instead so you end one call and join the next with a couple of clicks of your mouse. Enough time spent working within that culture and you start to treat it as normal. Taking a break for 5-10 minutes every hour or so sounds like an alien concept that you couldn't possibly achieve. You start to see breaks as non-productive time and think that if you eliminate the non-productive time and work through it means you can go home earlier which has got to be worth it right?

It took me many years of work-related stress to change my thinking on that and to be more protective of my time. I know on days when I have enforced taking short breaks that I finish the day with more energy and a lot less frazzled than on the days I don't take breaks. When I worked with Jo, she ensured her routine blocked out time in her Outlook calendar to focus solely on her project and also the necessary weekly review and thinking time. She protected those timeslots vigorously and as a result managed to give herself the space to work on her project.

Important or Urgent?

Another thing that really helped Jo was using an evaluation tool to help her decide whether something that came up at work was worth rescheduling her protected timeslots for. I had only seen it used inside the business world but with a little adaptation this same tool can be used for personal projects to assess whether something is worth adjusting your weekly routine for. The tool is a simple grid that compares how urgent something is with how important something is and identifies 4 sections:

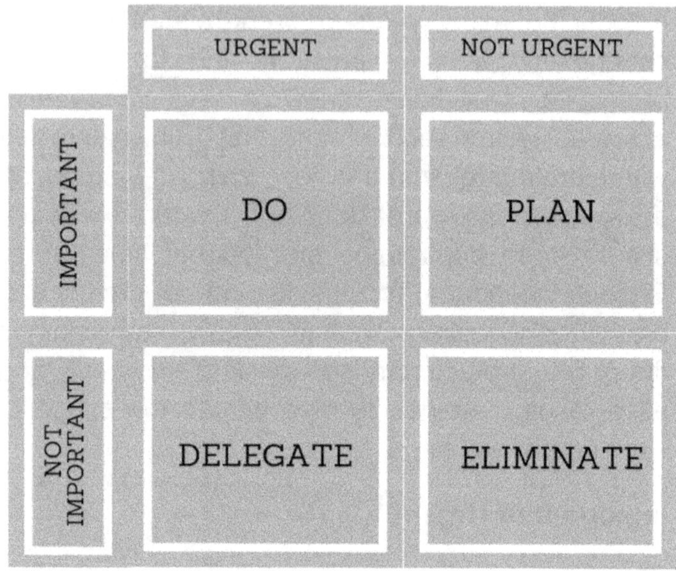

The way to use this grid is to take a moment to identify whether the new thing you are being asked to do is important to you and/or whether it is urgent for you.

Importance is defined as something with great significance or value.

Urgency is defined as requiring immediate action or attention.

• Things that are both urgent and important to you should be done and you may need to adjust your routine to accommodate them (box 1).

• Things that are important to you but not urgent should be added to your plan (box 2).

• Things that are not important to you but urgent none the less will need doing but you should find someone else to do them (box 3). For Jo these tasks were delegated to a member of her team, for your personal project this might be something you could ask a spouse to do or push the request back to the person making it to do as they are usually the one with the sense of urgency around the thing.

• Things that are neither important nor urgent simply don't get done (box 4).

Thinking in these terms can be a really simple way of helping you protect your time blocks and if you make a point of quickly assessing every new request that comes in to you it soon becomes habit.

Working consistently within your routine will enable you to make steady progress. This is important not only for success in your project but also in developing your sense of trust in yourself. Most people have a number of failed attempts at tackling new things or making positive change and that will erode your confidence and self-belief around actually being successful this time. Holding yourself accountable can be really hard. You know that if you fail to hit a deadline you've set or complete a task that you've scheduled for yourself, that you are the only person who needs to know that and that there is no obvious consequence for doing so.

The consequence that you don't immediately see is that you have broken your trust in yourself which makes it harder for you to believe that you will actually do what you have said you will do the next time. If this isn't a problem for you then that's great! However, if you recognise yourself in what I am describing here then you need to find a way that works for you to create that accountability to get things done. For example, if you know that you tend to put things off until your back is up against a wall with a hard deadline and then you pull out all the stops to deliver the thing, then go and build yourself a wall to put your back against. This could be getting someone else to set your deadlines. It could be finding an accountability partner who you call or meet with once a week to step through your weekly review and show them what you've done. It could be going public with what you are doing so that you don't look stupid if you then don't follow through and complete your project. Get to know yourself and what works for you towards taking action.

12 KEEPING TRACK

Now that you have worked out how to fit progressing your plan into your life, we will look at ways to track progress against your plan, how to undertake minor replanning when needed and how to handle small 'blips' in progress and get yourself back on track.

There are two aspects of your plan that you need to track:

1. Progress towards the end goal;

2. Task completion.

Both are important to success as it is perfectly possible to tick off all the tasks you have defined but still not actually reach your goal. That might sound impossible so let me give you a simple example to illustrate how this can happen. Imagine you have a goal to lose 10 lbs in 6 weeks. You decide to do this by eating yogurt for breakfast, soup for lunch and salad for dinner every day. You tick off each meal as you eat it (these are your tasks) and then eagerly step on the scales 6 weeks later and find that you have only lost 6 lbs - still good progress but you have not achieved the goal you had set so you aren't happy. If you had also measured progress towards the end goal, perhaps by weighing yourself once a week, then you would have identified that you weren't losing as much weight as you expected. You were ticking off all the tasks but were not on track to lose 10 lbs. Monitoring this would have enabled you to adjust your approach and tweak your tasks to enable you to hit your goal.

Similarly, it is really important to track your task execution as that will also give you an early indicator of whether or not reaching your goal is still possible. Sticking with the same example as before, if you had a week with lots of social commitments and ended up eating 100% of your breakfasts and lunches to plan but went off plan for 5 dinners that week (and had a few slices of birthday cake), unless you are tracking each task's completion, you are likely to forget or underestimate where you veered off plan. Knowing how many tasks have slipped, been rescheduled or missed altogether is a really powerful measurement as it can stop you sliding way off track. At a minimum you should be reviewing both the details of your task completion and progress towards your goal weekly. If you have a busy period where you have a lot of tasks to do in a given week to a deadline, then daily task tracking is better to enable you to catch any slips as early as possible.

The Weekly Review

The concept of a formal "weekly review" can sound a bit worrying if you aren't used to managing plans but it doesn't have to be complicated. In simple terms, during my weekly reviews I typically look at three things: what was planned for the week, what I managed to get done, and whether I am on track towards my goal. If I am running a large project which includes contributions from other people then they will be part of that review too but most of the time it's just me.

I use my weekly review to:

- Count how many of last week's tasks I completed, how many I rescheduled, and how many are open tasks (not yet complete).

- Assess the impact of any tasks I didn't complete. What has that done to any successors for those tasks.

- Tweak the plan for the coming week to compensate for any delay and stay on track.

- Review my Plan on a Page overview to

reconnect with my overall goal and to check that the rest of the project is still on track, adjusting the overview as necessary.,

- Review my list of project risks to see if they are still valid, if any have crept up on me during the week or if I have identified any new ones.

- Update my notes, schedule the upcoming week's tasks into my diary and that's it.

For a small project, this typically takes me about 15-20 minutes a week now that I've developed the habit of doing it. For larger projects that involve getting updates from other people, the review could take 45-60 minutes as I need to ensure everyone's tasks are tracked, updated and that they are all clear on what they are doing next week but it shouldn't take any longer than that to complete. So that these weekly reviews don't slip it is essential to have these as non-negotiable appointments with yourself and ensure that you get them done. If you don't review, you are much more likely to have things slip so the sooner you can build this habit the better!

Many people I work with will fit this review into their schedules in line with how they organise their first/last day of the week - so for example on a Sunday in preparation for starting the new week's tasks on a Monday but this is completely up to you when you do this. Don't feel that you need to do these reviews on a Sunday if that is a bad day for you. For me personally Sundays are usually so busy with other things that I don't have the time or inclination to plan my week. Instead I will plan on a Monday night right through to the following Monday as that works better for me. Feel free to do them any day that makes sense to you during the week - just make sure you do them!

Be consistent with the same day each week and build them into your weekly routine. If you feel that waiting to review each week isn't giving you the visibility on progress that you need then you can also schedule midweek or daily reviews as needed. Daily reviews would follow the same format as the weekly review that I outlined above, but would just track the previous day's tasks and confirm the planned tasks for the day ahead instead. I have found the most effective time of day for a daily review is first thing in the morning as it puts today's tasks front and centre in your mind for the day ahead and also gives you the whole day to work with if you need to catch up on any slipped tasks.

Dealing with Slips

If you identify any slipped or outstanding tasks during your review, you need to make some decisions about what you are going to do with them. The first thing to establish is whether you missed the task because it isn't actually important to the overall plan any more. This can happen as you start to work with your plan and your plan evolves from what you had originally created. An example from my Everest fundraising project was that I had scheduled a couple of tasks one week to investigate whether it would be feasible to host a fashion show at a local community centre or sports hall. However, earlier in the week I had some really exciting news that made the idea for a charity gig into a more solid prospect. If the charity gig ended up being a viable fundraiser then there would be no need to do the fashion show too, so I made the decision to not follow up on the fashion show tasks as they were no longer as important to my plan.

If you know that the task is still a valid one then more immediate decisions need to be made. In reality, for a personal project you are both managing the plan and doing the tasks so you will know that a task is slipping straight away. What needs to be established quickly is what the impact is of that task not being completed on time. You need to objectively look at the impact of the slippage rather than getting emotional about the reasons why it slipped. It is so easy to have a bad day that scuppers what you had planned to do. You had your schedule set, made sure everything was ready for action, and then wham! Something comes up. This could be a need to suddenly work late, a major traffic jam which means you get home 2 hours later than planned, one of your kids is sick, you have a really crappy day and all your focus on your goal goes out of the window. So what happens then?

Once you have looked after the ill person, or finally got out of the traffic, you are left with a choice - do you write off the day and replan, just pushing everything back a day? Or do you sit down anyway and take action? My advice is to ensure that you do something, anything that helps you move forward even a small amount. Remember any time you choose to work on completing a task then you are working towards your goal. Any time you choose to write off the day you are standing still and your goal will stay out of reach. If you aren't consistently making the decision to move yourself forward then you are consistently making the decision not to. Each day you push your plan back is a day lost. I am not casting judgement here, I am simply stating fact, but this is a fact that many people don't pay attention to until it's too late. You always have a choice over what you do.

Sometimes writing the day off is absolutely the right thing to have done. If you are faced with an unexpected short-term crisis such as looking after a sick relative, dealing with a home emergency of some kind or being ill yourself, then taking a break from your plan is the only thing you can do. If this happens to you then please be kind to yourself - I see so many people taking time out for genuine reasons and then basically guilt-tripping themselves about lack of progress on their plan and then diving straight into it again, frantically trying to catch up and causing themselves more stress. What you need to do in this situation is calm down and focus on replanning in the most effective way possible. If you try and shoe-horn the missed tasks into another day without giving yourself room to be able to do that then you are not going to succeed. Please don't try. If you over stretch yourself you are setting yourself up to fail and that will go on to create more problems with things like self-belief and your mindset. Guilt-tripping yourself also just adds unnecessary stress which then will impact your ongoing progress. Just tick days like that off as "rescheduled" and then spend the next available time you have working on replanning.

Sometimes, however, writing the day off is really just a convenient excuse - you could have done something today but you chose not to. It felt easier at the time to let today's tasks slide. After all what harm can one day make? You will be able to catch up again tomorrow right? You own your plan so you are empowered to make the decision for yourself about how you manage this but please do make an informed choice. If you don't manage to do all of the tasks that were planned then you will need to sit down as soon as possible and work out where you can plan in some additional time to get them completed so that your overall plan doesn't slip. It is really useful to track slippages as part of the weekly review as needing to do this a lot might mean that you need to build some extra flexibility into your plan to allow for unpredictable weeks.

> You have created a plan and chosen your planning tool.
>
> You have identified time gaps in your day you can use for your project.
>
> You have created a routine to make the most of your time.
>
> You have scheduled your Weekly Review sessions.

CREATE SUCCESS

13 DISASTER

For many people reading this book, this will not be the first time that you have decided to try and tackle a challenge that is holding you back in some way. You will have potentially tried and failed with a number of things before but if you have followed the steps in this book so far you will be armed with new tools to help you make a success of it this time. You have learnt to prioritise, identify tasks, create a plan and think about solutions to things that could go wrong before you start so that you can deal with them effectively. Having potentially been burned before, you may be sitting there saying to yourself "yes, yes, this is all very well, but what happens when it all goes wrong?" How would you recover from something that takes more than a little tweak of your plan to remedy? That is what this section is for - disaster recovery!

In my career, I have seen (and managed) a number

of projects that have gone pear-shaped! Sometimes this was due to poor initial planning, but more often this was due to known risks becoming a problem, or unforeseen events happening impacting the projects. The two elements to disaster recovery that I am going to cover in this section are:

- Proactive disaster recovery (heading risks off at the pass);

- Reactive disaster recovery (when an unexpected issue hits).

When a Risk Impacts

Earlier, you had identified some potential risks that might stop you reaching your goal. You also made some notes about things you could do to overcome the problem just in case it actually happened. As part of your weekly review you should be keeping an eye on these risks and reviewing to make sure they don't suddenly become a problem. So how do you do that effectively? At its simplest, you review each item that you identified as a potential risk and you see if the circumstances around it have changed since you looked at it last. Some questions you can consider:

- Is this risk still relevant or have you moved on with your plan enough that this risk no longer matters?

- Has it grown any less likely to happen?

- Has it grown any more likely to happen?

- Are there any things you need can do not or in the future to ensure this doesn't become a problem?

The last time I had to recover a near disaster was during my fundraising project. I had planned to hold a music event as a charity fundraiser with a few local bands playing in a local venue with the profits from ticket sales going towards my target. I worked closely with my husband on this project as he had a number of connections into the local music scene and between us we had identified a number of risks to holding this event. The main ones were not being able to sell enough tickets to make a profit, not being able to find a decent (but cheap!) venue and not having bands to play at the gig. We had worked out ways to overcome each of these and progressed with the project. My husband found a good venue at a favourable rate which had the added bonus of meaning we only had to sell 50 tickets to break even - anything after that then was profit towards the target. We had enlisted a number of friends, family and colleagues to help us sell tickets too so we were confident that we could sell more than 50. So far so good with 2 out of 3 of our main risks.

The risk we had been keeping an eye on was related to the bands. We had initial agreement from 3 bands to each to do a set on the night. One was quite a new band, the other two bands had featured on the local circuit for a number of years and would also bring a number of their own followers along for the night so all in all this was looking like it would be a successful event. We fixed a date with all 3 bands, had verbal confirmation they were fine to go ahead and so booked the venue. However, when we got the booking paperwork through from the venue a couple of weeks later, because they had offered us such a generous rate, they requested payment up front to secure it for us. This wasn't something we had expected and our immediate thought was that we then needed to make 100% sure that if we were going to lay down money for the room that the event went ahead. We asked each band to confirm in writing that they could definitely play on the night as previously agreed. The first band responded almost immediately that they could. The second band also confirmed, but the third band went radio-silent. No response to email, no response to voicemails, nothing. It looked like we would need to just offer two bands on the night, so we did some number-crunching and still thought we could make it work if we managed to get both bands playing longer sets.

The next day, my husband got a call from the second band - there was more bad news. They had been offered a slot to play at an industry event they had been trying to get into for months. The slot would put them in front of labels and agents and was a massive opportunity for them. And it was the same night as our charity gig… They would have been mad to turn down that opportunity so we wished them well and sadly crossed them off our list. It wasn't going to be viable to run the event with one inexperienced band, and the timescales in which the venue wanted the payment was too short for us to find good replacement bands so we decided that we had to cancel the gig.

Keeping a close eye on the risk around the bands had ensured we weren't landed with the expensive mistake of hiring a venue for nothing. I also had time to go back to the drawing board, dip into my contingency planning ideas and identify some alternative activities I could explore to make up the shortfall for what I had planned to raise from that event.

Control and management of the plan really helped me to mitigate the impact of losing the bands. I had no influence over what the bands decided to do but by focusing on things that I could control, rather than getting stressed about it, meant that I could proactively manage the impact that this had on my overall plan. I knew in advance that this was an area of risk, I had some high-level contingency plans in place and I had enough understanding of how this event fitted into my overall plan to be able to make an informed decision to let the gig go and move on to something else. Was it an emotional time? Yes absolutely! Having worked so hard on planning and moving the event forward from an idea into something (almost) real and getting really excited about how fun it would be and how much of an achievement, it came as quite a blow when things started to go wrong and it became clearer that it wasn't going to happen.

Disappointment tinged with panic is a really common emotion when your plans start to go wrong but in order to recover from setbacks you really need to take the emotion out of what you are doing (or at least park it to one side for a bit) whilst you replan and work out your next steps to move forward. By all means take a bit of time out to go and vent/hide/cry/eat chocolate - whatever works for you - then when you are ready, come back to your plan ready to look at how you can move forward. Staying trapped in that negative emotion will keep you stuck. You need to put it aside, out of your way, and then look rationally at what you can do next to get over the hurdle and move forward.

Out of the Blue

What happens when it isn't just the risks in your plan that go wrong but something completely unexpected blows your whole plan out of the water? This is what happened to Charlie. Charlie's goal was to set up his own martial arts based bootcamp classes at weekends as a side-line to his day job. He had been a keen martial artist for more than a decade and had a long-standing dream to teach martial arts for a living rather than continue to do his desk-based job until retirement. Having followed the same processes that you have in this book, Charlie had created a plan, had been following it for several months and was all geared up to actually launching his bootcamp business when disaster struck!

Charlie was competing in a martial arts tournament when he lost his focus during a jump spinning kick and landed awkwardly on the mat with a crunch. This resulted in a broken arm plus a torn muscle in his shoulder that required minor surgery - ouch! After treatment, he was fitted with a sturdy cast and arm brace that encompassed his arm and shoulder and pretty much immobilised them both. His doctor had said his arm would need to be in a cast for around 2 months for the bone to heal and after that he would need several months of physiotherapy before he could contemplate returning to martial arts or doing anything too physical - which was exactly what he needed to do for his new business.

This happened two weeks before Charlie's planned launch and he was devastated. He could see all that work, all that planning and his dream of running his own business just being washed away. He had no choice but to cancel his plans and have a think about what he was going to do. Charlie had initially thought about completely throwing in the towel and giving up on his plan altogether, after all what could he do for the next few months -

absolutely nothing. He felt that he would be so far behind on his plan that it would be pointless trying to pick it up again.

Charlie wallowed for a few days then decided he'd look over his notes and plans. He spent some time reconnecting with the reasons why he wanted to start his business in the first place and reviewed all his ideas and remembered how excited he had felt once he'd finally decided on his direction and started planning it all out. He looked again at his mind maps and his list of tasks and started to think about how many of these he might still be able to move forward with or adapt in some way to work around his restricted mobility for the next few months. He brainstormed this out into a new mind map and could see some potential ways he could still move his business idea forward whilst he was recovering. He also started to think about people he could find to help him with some of the tasks and started to think about a different way to position the launch of his business. He also began to focus on what he could do rather than what he couldn't - he was still able to use a computer and a phone so could start finding new clients that way rather than in person as he had first planned.

Charlie could have decided his plan was beyond rescue and given up, but with some time to think about how he could approach it in a different way, he overcame the setback from his injury and is still able to move his plan forward - just more slowly.

Most project disasters can be recoverable in the same way given some time to think again around the problem and some replanning to get to an outcome that still works for you.

Throwing your own spanner in the works

One thing that I have seen fatally sabotage personal projects is giving in to internal self-doubt and talking yourself out of success. When something goes wrong it is really easy to get caught out by that little voice in your head and feel like you can't do it and you need to give up. This holds true at any point during your project including when you might least expect it - when the end is nearly in sight and you can almost taste success. Fear of success can be just as responsible for you stopping your own progress as fear of failure. Be mindful and aware of when you feel either one of those creep in.

There is a concept called "minimum effective dose" that really comes into its own when things have hit a sticky patch and it is also great for helping you work through fear to keep moving forward. The concept is basically identifying and then completing the smallest version of a task each day or each week that will still help to keep your plan ticking over.

Looking at how the minimum effective dose can come in useful, Sam is in training for his charity run and something comes up at work which means he needs to work late every night for a week. He now does not have time to go out and run the three 4 mile runs that were scheduled for this week on his training plan. Sam doesn't want to skip a week on the plan but knows his available time is being squeezed so he decides to just run for 1 mile instead on each of his planned running days but make it a bit faster than his usual pace figuring that will still be useful for his fitness. So that is what he does. He can then just make some minor adjustments to his training plan for the following week and be back on track. What can you identify as the minimum effective dose for your project? Stick to the process - plan, do, review - and you will continue to make progress towards your goal.

Your Plan v Other People

As you start to make real change in your life and real progress towards your goals, you may find this has an unexpected impact on some of your relationships. People you had assumed would be supportive of your plans and who you thought would help you may behave in the completely opposite way and become your strongest critic. They will find fault with your plan, fault with why you are trying to make changes and will try to convince you that nothing you do will ever work. It doesn't matter if they are close friends, family or colleagues, other people in your life can put up a surprising amount of resistance to the change you are trying to make.

If you are surrounded by negative people when you are trying to move forward with your project, it can be really tough. You need to be crystal clear on why you are doing what you are doing and make a conscious decision not to take other people's comments and criticism onboard. Most of the time there is no actual problem with you or with your project. It is simply that what you are doing has triggered off something inside them that is making them feel uncomfortable and they are projecting that discomfort back onto you. Learning to not take their comments on board is the best way you can deal with them.

If you feel like you are always surrounded by people who are continually negative and holding you back then go and look for support elsewhere. There has never been an easier time to find and connect with like-minded people. You could find a coach or a mentor to help you manage the tough times and encourage you to keep moving forward. You could join an online group on a social media platform like Facebook or LinkedIn or you could join a club or Meetup group that is related to your goals so that you can make friends with some new people who understand what you are trying to do and can therefore offer support. Having a handful of people that you can turn to really makes all the difference so that you don't feel like you are on your own.

14 YOU V YOU

Change is hard, really hard. Not in the obvious sense that something like running 100 consecutive marathons would be hard for most people. Hard because change requires not only overcoming your inertia to take the first step in a new direction but then following that up with continual consistent action until the change you aspired to becomes your new normal. You can have the most inspiring personal goals, a great big "why" to spur you on and the best action plan in the universe, but none of that is any use unless you actually go and do the things you need to do to get to where you want to go.

What I see time and time again is people who start all fired up doing something new and exciting. They set a goal, start working towards it and then it just fizzles. They lose focus, lose momentum and just stop. For personal development projects, it is rarely an external risk that jumps up to sabotage them, nor a major disaster that knocks them off their game. They just find that their initial burst of enthusiasm has waned and before they even consciously realise it, they have stopped doing the things that they had said they would. They slip back into old habits and old routines. What happened? Fear kicked in and they simply sabotaged themselves.

I know this story well as I have been that person so many times. I have discussed fear already and how it can sneak up on you and limit your thinking, cloud your judgement and disguise itself as common sense so I won't repeat that here. What I am going to cover in this section is how I manage my fear when it taps me on the shoulder so that I still manage to get things done despite my own best efforts to stop myself.

Why do we keep trying to stop ourselves moving forward? For you to have come this far you have overcome your resistance to change a number of times already - in deciding what you wanted to focus on, in setting yourself a goal, in creating a plan and in starting to execute it. Even many weeks or months into your plan you need to be vigilant as you will keep trying to derail yourself. All of this comes back to parts of our brains being afraid of change and trying to keep us safe by any means possible.

Have you ever watched children who are siblings

interact for any length of time, or do you have brothers or sisters yourself? You can usually see that one child can move the other from calm and happy to absolutely irate in seconds. They have learnt from a young age exactly what to say or do to the other person to provoke that reaction. I know that I can still do this to my brother in about 10 seconds flat, and we are both grown now with families of our own!

Everyone has triggers or has areas of their life that they are particularly sensitive to being prodded. Anything that presses those mental buttons guarantees a response. Now think of yourself in those same terms - you have You and Inner You who can act very much like siblings, they generally get on but don't always see eye to eye. In terms of your personal projects, You has the goal and is driving forward, Inner You is scared of the change that the project could mean for you. Both You and Inner You have grown up together so Inner You knows exactly what buttons to press on You to get the reaction that Inner You is looking for, i.e. to stop you changing so you stay safely as you were before. Inner You has no scruples and will use them all! How this manifests will vary from person to person and plan to plan but what is common to all situations is that Inner You is highly skilled at manipulating You to throw You off track.

My Inner You has a pattern whenever I start something new:

Stage 1: "You don't know what you are doing, this will never work".

This brings out all of the self-doubt and fear about even thinking of making a change. Spending time going through the exercises I mentioned earlier to get clear on my direction and priorities really helps me get my self-talk under control enough to start thinking that this is something I could actually do.

Stage 2: "People like you can't do things like that"

This is all about me scaling up. I do have real trouble sometimes looking at my biggest vision for the things I want to achieve. The way I have managed to get through that is by following a smaller version of the process I have outlined in this book - start by visualising a level that both me and Inner Rachel are comfortable with and then I break down various elements of that vision and show myself how the thing is possible just by turning them up a bit. For example, going from little exercise to trekking to Everest Base Camp on the face of it my Inner Rachel was nearly shouting that "People like you can't do that" but by breaking this down into its component parts - essentially it is mostly walking - then I can see it in a way that my Inner Rachel stops having a panic about:

Me:
I know I can walk

Inner Rachel:
Yes but this will be for several hours at a time.

Me:
I have done things like this before you know!

Inner Rachel:
Yes but you were much younger then.

Me:
I have a 10 month training plan to make sure I'm prepared.

Inner Rachel:
Yes but it will be difficult!

Me:
So I'm not that old and will be well prepared. Any other reason I can't do this trek?

Inner Rachel:
Erm, I guess not...

Whenever I have changed something in my life - new career, moving to a new area, starting up a new venture - I go through the same process as above to get through stage 2 and that usually generates enough confidence to keep Inner Rachel quiet for a bit!

<u>Stage 3</u>: "Not so fast!"

The next stage Inner Rachel chimes in is during the execution of my plan. She brings 3 friends along to this one - Distraction, Procrastination and Comparison.

Distraction

Distraction is something that interrupts what you are trying to do. People often think of this as something quite obvious like someone walking up to talk to you when you are trying to concentrate but more often in our "always on" world, distractions are tiny little things like that flashing notification icon on your phone which prompt an irresistible urge to just go and check it out for a few seconds. Can't hurt right? Have you ever noticed how a quick scroll through your Facebook timeline or a catch up on what's new on Twitter or Instagram starts out with the intention of just being a couple of minutes but before you know it, the best part of an hour has gone by?

That quick check can very quickly eat up the time you had put aside to work on something within your action plan. I know I am guilty of this. Even though I am aware of the distraction potential of having my smartphone anywhere near me or Internet access when I am trying to concentrate I do still find myself reaching for my phone or opening a web browser almost without thinking. When I'm writing, Inner Rachel quite often positions that quick check as "research" for the topic I am writing about to make it even more irresistible - sometimes she wins, sometimes I do!

Your distraction of choice might not be social media but you will have something that tempts you. This might be going to make endless cups of tea or coffee (can't work without a fresh drink right?), remembering a "super-urgent" job like watering the plants, walking the dog, filing your nails, or, like one client of mine, brushing and braiding her hair… You will need to take a look at what it is that you do. Pay attention to yourself and your actions when you sit down to work and find your thing. Once you have identified it then you can work on noticing yourself doing it. Notice yourself doing it enough times and you can look at ways to break the habit and resolve it.

When I realised what I was doing, when I really need to knuckle down I leave my phone in another room and disable the Wi-Fi on my laptop. That forces me to then concentrate on what I actually need to be doing. A "quick Google" is then a trip across the house to go get my phone, or heading into the settings on my laptop to turn it back on. Both of these require conscious effort and not just opening a browser on autopilot. This simple action has been effective enough to keep me on track. (In case you were curious, for my client who braided her hair, her simple action was to change where she worked at home so she wasn't in sight of a mirror. No view of her hair meant she then didn't develop a sudden urge to braid it - distraction removed!)

Procrastination

Procrastination and distraction are closely related with one often feeding the other. Allowing distractions to stop you moving forward with your plan is a form of procrastination, as is trying to research to an infinite level of detail, having no deadline so perpetually starting next Monday, rearranging your pen collection while you decide where to start - there are many ways to procrastinate too! Years of analysing my own behaviour helped me to identify that I would also procrastinate by being overly helpful to others. I would readily pick up their urgent (but not always important) tasks and push back my own plans and projects to help them achieve theirs.

What really helped me break that behaviour pattern was to make sure I was crystal clear on

1. Why I had started my project in the first place, and

2. What achieving it would mean to me.

I built a new habit of reminding myself of these two things daily (Dory time!) so that they were at the forefront of my mind when a potential procrastination opportunity cropped up. Having that reminder fresh in my head made it a lot easier for me to be able to prioritise and ultimately make more progress on my projects.

The other thing that helped me overcome procrastination was better planning. For every task and timeslot I have on my plan, I have a very clear understanding of what I want to achieve.   I recognised that sometimes I would sit down to work on my next task and I would not feel 100% sure of what I was to do at that point. That would usually open the door to distraction as I tried to fix my knowledge gap with more information. The first thing that I would find myself doing is reaching for my phone for that quick Google as I mentioned earlier and before I realise I would have lost an hour...

On tracking and analysing my own behaviour, I found that if I took a moment to review the upcoming tasks ahead of time and check how clear my understanding was then I could usually identify which ones I didn't feel fully prepared for. I started to build this quick check into my weekly review so now if I do come across a task that I feel like I am not fully prepared for, I take some time to do that piece of prep or split the task down further into a prep task and a do task so that when it comes to the doing part I can just crack on and do it.

Comparison

Another thing that can give you some trouble when you embark on a personal project is an affliction called "Comparisonitis". No need to seek medical attention, this is caused by looking at what you are doing and comparing yourself and your efforts to someone else and what they have achieved. Invariably you will end up looking at the other person and deciding what they have done is amazing and what you have done is rubbish. It becomes a problem when you find yourself comparing where you are to where they are and find yourself lacking. You lose faith and confidence in yourself and how far you have come and get discouraged around continuing.

I have seen this behaviour occur in every client I have had and most people that I meet. It is also another of my specialities where I have years of experience! If you have ever said something like "yep I do such and such but I'm not as good as Fred" then that's what I am talking about. You then start to allow Inner You to berate you with a whole load of "shoulds" - I should be doing this or should be doing that. Take care that doesn't spiral down and encourage you to give up.

I can still slip into the comparison trap from time to time - my drive to make sure I do the best that I can on my projects means that I hold myself to high standards and will tend to focus on my weaknesses and unfairly compare my weaknesses to their successes. It is not a fair comparison to comparing yourself to someone way ahead of you. If your goal is to run a 10k and it takes you 72 minutes the first time (that was my very first timed run) then you need to use that as your own line in the sand to improve upon - not look at Mo Farah running it in 26 minutes and think you are rubbish. What does help is remembering that even the super successful ones do the same thing and compare themselves to people who are on the next rung of the ladder - the difference is that they use this comparison to set new goals rather than hold themselves back.

More rarely you might be someone with sky-high confidence and think what you are doing is much better than anything else you have seen anyone else do. You clearly have it all nailed so, like the story of the tortoise and the hare, you start to get complacent and take your foot off the gas. You find your plan and project slip and you don't achieve what you set out to, but you can't really work out why. This has never been me but I have seen it happen to people through my career who are brilliant at what they do but just end up fizzling out.

In order to succeed, you need to build small positive habits and focus solely on moving yourself forward. Don't worry about what anyone else is doing, just focus on you, your journey and being better than you were yesterday.

15 SUCCESS

You have done it! Achieved your goal, reached your target, ticked all the tasks off your list - well done!

In this final section let's talk about what happens when you get to this point - the end of your project. Two things are absolutely essential: reviewing your project and celebrating success.

ASK how it went

The End of Project Review helps you tidy up the loose ends, digest what you achieved and record what you have learned from the whole project and project process. Get into the habit of doing them for every single project you do - no matter how small - as they can bring out some really valuable lessons. The review can be as detailed or as simple as you want so don't think of this as a difficult thing to do. I normally start with three high level categories to capture information about my projects and then I add notes where needed if there is something in particular that I really want to record. My high-level categories are:

> **Avoid** (what you don't want to do again, what really didn't work).

> **Sharpen** (what you would improve or do better next time).

> **Keep** (what went well and what you would do the same way again).

I usually take a sheet of paper and divide it simply into quarters. I label each quarter with either Avoid, Sharpen, Keep or Notes and then write down everything I can think of that fits into each of these categories into the relevant section. For small projects this can take about 10-15 minutes, for larger projects this can take about 30 minutes so the overall process is really quite quick. To give you an idea of the types of things I capture, here are some examples from my cake sale:

> **Avoid** - e.g. next time don't buy bulk stock before seeing what sells well - we ended up with about 48 bottles of water left over as everyone wanted the cans of cola and lemonade.

> **Sharpen** - e.g. use cool boxes to keep temperature stable for the cakes/fudge as

things were getting a bit sticky, locate nearer the entrance of the hall we were in as people had to come all the way in to find us, prepare more in advance (non-baking things) as we had late nights before the sales getting everything ready.

Keep - e.g. individual portion packing was really good and made it easy to transport & display product and made purchasing quick and easy for the consumer, we made our target money for each cake sale, we raised awareness for the trek, we got repeat customers at follow-on events, we were able to also sell raffle tickets, adding pre-packaged pic 'n mix sold really well.

If my project has been one related to personal change, I also add in some notes about how I feel around the change I made - what I felt like before, and what it feels like now. This piece I keep handy or bookmark that page in my journal so I can re-read it if I feel like old habits are slipping back in. I keep my Review materials in a folder (a physical one!) or in my bullet journal and I do make a habit to look over them when I am looking to start doing a similar project in future, particularly to add any relevant Avoids and Sharpens to my risk list for the new project.

Celebrate!

The final piece of the process before you can finally

close the door on your project is celebrating your success. You might be surprised to hear that in my experience this is something that a lot of people really struggle with however it really is a necessary part of your journey and will also help to keep you on track.

Some countries are much better at rewarding success than others as it is embedded in their culture. I spent a lot of time working for large American corporations with a multinational presence and the differences between different countries can be striking. When I worked at Hewlett-Packard, the employee reward system was set up to allow you to record and send a short video of thanks to a colleague for doing a great job, plus things like long service awards had their own package of posters and fanfare music that could be downloaded from the intranet and used to surprise the awardee at their desk. You could also send a very innocuous e-card instead.

My American colleagues loved the fanfare and the video messaging and found a lot of creative ways to use them to celebrate both individual and team success.

My British colleagues would have cheerfully flayed themselves alive rather than have a fanfare drawing attention to them in the office and were much more likely to send a modest e-card instead.

The same cultural differences were evident when

celebrating successes at the end of a project or the small wins along the way - a lot of "good job!" on the American-led team meetings and the occasional understated "well done" on the British ones. It always amused me to observe this as although most people don't like to think they adhere to a national stereotype, those traits are certainly evident in many of us! I don't know if it is as a result of the "British Reserve" or just a general national mindset in the UK but in my experience, British people can have real difficulty owning and celebrating their successes.

The main reason for making such a big deal around celebrating your success is that it encourages you to recognise the sustained effort you have put in to reach your goal. If you don't mark it in some way then it does just become something that you did once and loses its importance. You will find yourself either forgetting what you achieved or worse, starting to think of it in terms of "what you should have done". You know this thinking is starting to creep in if you find yourself saying things like "I did xyz, but..." or "it was only xyz" and downplaying all the work you put in and all that you achieved.

On my Everest trek I was pretty much the slowest walker in the group so was often at the back of the pack. I could give myself a hard time about not being as fast or as fit as some of the others in the group but in the end does that detract from what I achieved? Nope. Focus on the big goal that you achieved - if you lost 30 lbs in 6 months then celebrate that you lost 30 lbs rather than undermining all that amazing work because you wanted to lose 32 lbs in that period. It is only you that will sweat the details. In 18 years of working on projects, both professionally and personally, I have never seen one that has been 100% perfect in the end - there is usually a list of minor snags that need to be finished off but on the whole the outcome was achieved. Treat your near misses (like that final 2 lb) in the same way - just as small snags to be picked up later, and don't let them devalue what you achieved overall.

As celebrating my successes has been an area I have always struggled with, I devoted some time to learn how to overcome it and learn how to reward myself. I got the general idea and the logic behind it - create a positive experience by rewarding your achievements and that will encourage you to carry on to achieve more. For years the nearest I got to a reward system for myself was basically a form of bribery - I would buy a nice box of chocolates and then if I knuckled down and did the thing I had been putting off (studying for that exam/writing that document/making that phonecall) I would reward myself with one chocolate from the box. That system worked for me for a few years until I got fed up of chocolate (yes really!) and until I started doing bigger personal projects where, quite frankly, a chocolate wasn't really cutting it in terms of providing motivation! I stopped rewarding myself and just got on with things. I wasn't going to stop setting myself personal projects and although I did carry on and complete them, it all began to feel pretty pointless. I tried to sell myself on the outcome of the project being its own reward which didn't always work so I decided to look into other non-chocolatey ways of celebrating success and started looking at what other people did.

In the corporate world, it is quite common to have an end of project night out or a group meal to thank everyone involved for successfully delivering a large project. You can use the same philosophy for your own personal projects and go out with some of the people who supported you through your project to celebrate. If you achieved your project on your own but still want to celebrate then that is absolutely fine - you can just organise a night out with friends but be the only one who realises why!

Alternatively, you could decide to reward yourself with something you have wanted to buy yourself for a while. Sam does this and uses part of his weekly review to think about the treat he's going to get himself when he completes his charity run project. He reviews his training progress that week and then transfers a fixed amount of money (£5) into his savings account if he's done all of his planned runs for the week and a lower amount of money (£3) if he's completed most of the runs but had a few challenges. He keeps a training spreadsheet and has added a tab to keep track of how much money he's got in his Treat Pot. Once his running event is over, he's going to take the Treat Pot and spend it on something he wants as a reward for consistent effort towards his goal.

If going out isn't really your thing or you aren't motivated by buying more stuff, then you can get more creative around what you can reward yourself with. I have worked with people who have used the same concept as Sam's Treat Pot but filled it with time rather than money - 5 or 10 minutes of guilt-free time to themselves for good progress each week and they'd then "spend" that however they liked - going out for the day, Netflix binge or a long lie in one weekend. You need to find something that is really going to work for you and you are going to appreciate after putting all that work in on your project - get creative! For my Everest trek my reward was a stay in a nice hotel in Kathmandu for a couple of days which allowed me to have a long soak in a bath (which was amazing after being grubby for 2 weeks) and to sleep in a bed with sheets rather than in a sleeping bag - absolute bliss! Whatever you decide to do, just make sure you decide to do at least something! You deserve it.

Now all you need to do is decide what you are going to do next??

AFTERWORD

This book has given you the tools I have distilled out of a career based on solving problems for other people. From coaching my staff, colleagues and senior management, to unravelling and solving business challenges – I have experienced many "fun and exciting learning opportunities" (which is how I like to refer, in polite company, to some of the things I have had to sort out over the years!). I am by far my own best customer as I have followed my own process a number of times now to make changes in my own life. I sincerely hope that you too can find the contents of this book of use when pursuing your own dreams.

If you want to connect, you can find me online at:
fb.me/racheljoneswrites
https://www.instagram.com/racheljoneswrites/

WITH THANKS

Thanks always to my wonderful husband Les for his universal support, large doses of common sense and many cups of tea to keep me going. Thanks also to Rhys and Evan for not minding too much when I spent long tranches of time typing into the night to get this book finished. We all know I only really let you win every game of Rocket League to make you both feel better! *wink* This book is for the three of you. Love you with all that I have x

Thanks to Phil Jones for helping me find the courage to embark on a writing career. Stumbling across your work in May 2016 has been life-changing in ways that you cannot imagine. Keep being your brilliant self.

Thanks to Shari Teigman for helping me find my inner maverick stitch the final pieces of my dream together.

Thanks to Joy Hopgood-Gravett, Poppy Brytewood, Ali Holloway, Sarah McGowan and Liam Hook for both beta-reading and your ongoing excitement about this project – it really did help me to keep going along the right path.

Thanks to my dad, David, for being the driving force behind my Everest experience. I hope you could see me from your cloud. Love and miss you always x

Lastly, thanks to my mum, Anne, for being the finest example of someone who is always looking for ways she can use her skills to help others. Love you x